Oxford International Primary History

5

Peter Rebman

Oxford International Primary for enquiring minds

Great Clarendon Street, Oxford, OX2 6DP, United Kingdom

Oxford University Press is a department of the University of Oxford. It furthers the University's objective of excellence in research, scholarship, and education by publishing worldwide. Oxford is a registered trade mark of Oxford University Press in the UK and in certain other countries.

The moral rights of the author have been asserted.

First published in 2017

All rights reserved. No part of this publication may be reproduced, stored in a retrieval system, or transmitted, in any form or by any means, without the prior permission in writing of Oxford University Press, or as expressly permitted by law, by licence or under terms agreed with the appropriate reprographics rights organization. Enquiries concerning reproduction outside the scope of the above should be sent to the Rights Department, Oxford University Press, at the address above.

You must not circulate this work in any other form and you must impose this same condition on any acquirer.

British Library Cataloguing in Publication Data
Data available

ISBN 978-0-19-841813-9

10 9 8 7 6 5 4 3 2

Paper used in the production of this book is a natural, recyclable product made from wood grown in sustainable forests. The manufacturing process conforms to the environmental regulations of the country of origin.

Printed in India by Manipal Technologies Limited

Acknowledgements

Cover: Carlo Molinari

Artwork: Aptara

Photos: p4 & p5: meunierd/Shutterstock; **p5 (L), p21 (BL) & p37 (L):** Algol/Shutterstock; **p5 (M), p21 (BM) & p37 (M):** ensiferum/Shutterstock; **p5 (R), p21 (BR) & p37 (R):** Algol/Shutterstock; **p6 & p18:** Regien Paassen/Shutterstock; **p7 & p19:** 3drenderings/Shutterstock; **p15:** Rolf Richardson/Alamy; **p15 (L):** Arcaid Images/Alamy; **p20, p21 & p30 (R):** World History Archive/Alamy ; **p21 (TL):** Prisma Archivo/Alamy; **p21 (TR):** Universal History Archive/UIG/Getty; **p30 (L):** LEON NEAL/Getty; **p31 (L):** Leemage/Getty; **p31 (R):** Geography Photos/Getty; **p37 & p37:** Anton_Ivanov/Shutterstock; **p38:** Olga Kot Photo/Shutterstock; **p39 (L):** Chamille White/Shutterstock; **p39 (R):** Kara Grubis/Shutterstock; **p41:** Anna Om/Shutterstock; **p42:** BERTRAND GUAY/Getty; **p43 & p50 (L):** K_Boonnitrod/Shutterstock; **p44:** Universal History Archive/Getty; **p46:** DEA/G. DAGLI ORTI/Getty; **p47 & p50 (R):** UniversalImagesGroup/Getty; **p48 (T):** soft_light/Shutterstock; **p48 (B):** Jannis Tobias Werner/Shutterstock; **p49:** Olga Kolos/Alamy; **p52 (L), p62 & p67 (TL):** ullstein bild/Getty; **p52 (TR):** ArchMan/Shutterstock; **p52 (BR) & p59:** Leemage/Getty; **p53 (B):** MATT CAMPBELL/Getty; **p53 (TL):** Faraways/Shutterstock; **p53 (TR), p57 & p66:** Julie Clopper/Shutterstock; **p55:** LianeM/Shutterstock; **p56 (L):** 44W-1384/Houghton Library/Harvard University; **p56 (R):** Bettmann/Getty; **p58 (BL) & (BR):** Drents Museum; **p58 (TL) & p67 (TR):** Francesco Dazzi/Shutterstock; **p58 (TR) & p67 (MR):** Awe Inspiring Images/Getty; **p60 (TR):** Sueddeutsche Zeitung Photo/Mary Evans; **p60 (BL):** Mary Evans Picture Library; **p61 & p67 (BL):** cyo bo/Shutterstock; **p64:** REX/Shutterstock; **p65:** Joel_420/Shutterstock

Although we have made every effort to trace and contact all copyright holders before publication this has not been possible in all cases. If notified, the publisher will rectify any errors or omissions at the earliest opportunity.

Links to third party websites are provided by Oxford in good faith and for information only. Oxford disclaims any responsibility for the materials contained in any third party website referenced in this work.

Contents

1 Roman invasion

1.1	Army and empire	6
1.2	The Romans invade	8
1.3	Roman settlers	10
1.4	Life in the Roman army	12
1.5	What was a Roman villa like?	14
1.6	The end of the Roman Empire	16
1 Review		18

2 The Anglo-Saxons

2.1	Who were the Anglo-Saxons?	22
2.2	Who ruled the Anglo-Saxons?	24
2.3a	What was life like in an Anglo-Saxon village?	26
2.3b	What was life like in an Anglo-Saxon village?	28
2.4	What were the achievements of the Anglo-Saxons?	30
2.5	Viking invasions	32
2 Review		34

3 The Maya

3.1	Who were the Maya?	38
3.2	What were Mayan cities like?	40
3.3	Who ruled the Maya?	42
3.4	Mayan merchants	44
3.5a	What achievements are the Maya known for?	46
3.5b	What achievements are the Maya known for?	48
3 Review		50

4 A history of transport

4.1a	On the road	54
4.1b	On the road	56
4.2	Water transport	58
4.3	Rail transport	60
4.4	Up in the air	62
4.5	Transport in the future	64
4 Review		66

Vocabulary quiz 68
Glossary 70

1 Roman invasion

In this unit you will:
- explore how and why the Romans invaded new lands
- describe what life was like in the Roman army
- explain how the Romans built their forts and towns
- describe what a Roman house looked like
- evaluate reasons why the Roman Empire declined

Key
- 265 BCE
- 202 BCE
- 30 BCE
- 117 CE

The growth of the Roman Empire

The Romans were based in the city of Rome in Italy. About 2000 years ago, the Romans ruled over an **empire** that covered most of Europe, North Africa and the Middle East. The Romans used their powerful army to **invade** large areas of land and **conquer** the people living there. The Roman army was the biggest and the best in the world.

empire invade conquer

? Look at the map.
1 Which was the only country controlled by the Romans in 265 BCE? ✓
2 List all the countries that the Romans had added to their empire by 30 BCE.
3 List the countries that the Romans added to the Roman Empire between 30 BCE and 117 CE.

The Romans
c500 BCE–476 CE

The (height of the) Maya
c250 CE–900 CE

The Anglo-Saxons
c400 CE–1066 CE

500 BCE   1100 BCE

1 Roman invasion

1.1 Army and empire

The strength of the Roman army allowed the Roman Empire to expand and conquer new lands. The Roman soldiers were better trained and had better weapons than the tribes they fought against. When the Romans defeated a tribe, they added the tribe's land to the Roman Empire. Which lands did the Romans conquer? How was the Roman army organised? What special weapons did the Roman army use?

The Roman Empire

The Roman Empire was one of the largest empires the world had ever known. The capital city Rome, in Italy, was the largest city in the world for 500 years between 100 BCE and 400 CE. In total, the Romans ruled over an estimated 50–90 million people, which was about 25 per cent of the world's population. Many modern countries and territories were included in the Roman Empire: much of Europe, including most of Britain (Scotland was not included), France, Germany, Italy, Spain, Portugal, Austria, Switzerland, Belgium, Greece, Hungary, Ukraine; the coastal area of northern Africa around the Mediterranean Sea (such as Libya, Tunisia, Algeria, Morocco, Egypt); the Balkans (such as Albania, Bosnia, Slovenia, Croatia, Bulgaria) and parts of the Middle East (such as Syria, Lebanon, Iraq, Jordan).

How the Roman army was organised

There were about 300 000 soldiers in the Roman army. The soldiers were divided into groups called legions.

Glossary words

ballista	century
battering ram	legion
cavalry	onager
centurion	

A legion contained about 5000 soldiers. The legions were split into groups of 80 and each group was called a century. The man in charge of a century was called a centurion. The century was then split into ten groups of eight soldiers, who shared a tent together.

In battle, the Romans protected themselves by grouping together and holding their shields above their heads. This was called the 'testudo' – a Latin word for 'tortoise'.

Did you know?

A Roman soldier marched so much that he wore out three pairs of boots each year!

How did the soldiers fight?

The soldiers fought in a tightly packed group. They marched slowly towards the enemy, holding their shields in front of them for protection. When the enemy threw rocks or spears at them, they lifted their shields above their heads for protection. When they got near to the enemy, the soldiers threw their spears, took out their swords and ran at the enemy. They sometimes used cavalry (soldiers on horses) to hunt down enemy soldiers who ran away.

What special weapons did the Romans use?

The Roman army sometimes had to conquer a town surrounded by a strong stone wall or a well-defended fortress. Then the army used larger weapons such as the ballista, the battering ram and the onager.

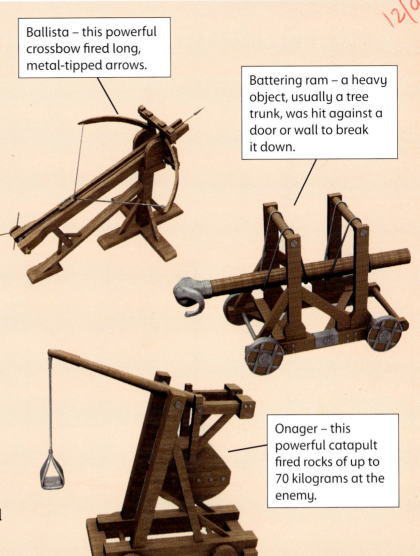

Ballista – this powerful crossbow fired long, metal-tipped arrows.

Battering ram – a heavy object, usually a tree trunk, was hit against a door or wall to break it down.

Onager – this powerful catapult fired rocks of up to 70 kilograms at the enemy.

Activities

1. Write a description of how the Roman army was organised. Include the words 'legion' and 'century' in your description.
2. Imagine you have joined the Roman army. Write a letter home explaining:
   a why you decided to join
   b how you fight in battles
   c the special weapons and equipment you use.

Challenge

Work with a partner or in a small group. Use books or the Internet to find out about some of the Roman army's most famous battles. Choose one battle and write a fact file about it. Base your fact file on the following questions. Who was the Roman emperor at the time? Why did the battle take place? Where was the battle? Who won – and how? Present your fact file to the rest of the class or include it as part of a class display.

1.2 The Romans invade

About 2000 years ago, tribes of people known as Celts ruled Britain. Then the Romans decided to invade Britain. The Romans had already captured vast areas of land around the Mediterranean Sea, Western Europe and parts of the Middle East. Why did the Romans invade Britain? Did they conquer the whole country? How successful were the Celts when fighting the Romans?

In Roman times, the area of Britain now known as Scotland was called Caledonia, and the people were known as the Caledonians. The Romans never defeated these fierce warrior tribes.

The Romans built Hadrian's Wall across England to keep watch and help defend against attacks.

Tribes hiding in the forests and hills fought fiercely against the Romans for many years. The Romans built many forts in these areas and placed large groups of soldiers where some of the fiercest tribes lived.

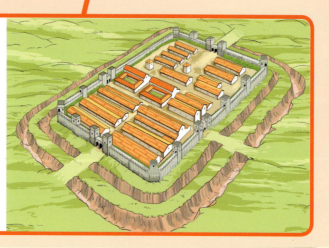

The southern part of Britain was the most peaceful. Over time, the Celts and the Romans mixed more and more.

'There are many men, buildings and herds of animals. There is much wood. The money is bronze or gold.'

This was written by a Roman emperor after a visit to Britain.

'Britain is at the very end of the earth. The Britons are savage towards foreigners. The seas around Britain are full of sea-monsters.'

This was written by a Roman poet in the 1st century BCE. He had not visited Britain.

Glossary words

Celts   goods   tribe

Why did the Romans invade Britain?

The Roman emperor at the time of the invasion was called Claudius. He wanted to show that he was a strong leader. He was unhappy that some of the Celts had been helping tribes in France fight against the Romans. The Romans were also looking for resources such as land, iron, lead, zinc, copper, silver and gold. When the Romans conquered new lands they gained control of all the goods and resources. The Romans then bought and sold the resources or took them back to Italy. For example, the Romans got olive oil, honey, pottery, marble and horses from Greece. They got corn, dates and figs from Egypt and perfumes, spices and jewels from the Middle East.

The invasion

The Romans invaded Britain in 43 CE. They landed on the south coast and fought many battles with different tribes of Celts. The Romans pushed the Celts back and captured the south of England within four years. In the north of England and in Wales there were thick forests and hills where the Celts could hide. It took the Romans another 30 years to conquer these parts.

Did you know?

The invasion of 43 CE was the third time the Romans invaded Britain. The first time, the Romans left because their ships were ruined in a storm. In the second invasion, the Romans beat many of the British tribes. However, the Romans eventually left Britain when the tribes promised to pay money to Rome each year.

The Celts fight back

Some Celts accepted Roman rule, but others still fought to try to make the Romans leave. In 60 CE, Queen Boudicca of the Celtic Iceni tribe gathered a huge army and burned several Roman towns in the south of England, including London, while the main part of the Roman army was in Wales. The Roman army quickly returned and attacked Boudicca's army. The Romans were outnumbered, but they were better organised and better equipped. Both sides lost many soldiers, but the Romans eventually won.

Activities

1. Why did the Romans decide to invade Britain?
2. How do the writers of the two written sources at the bottom of page 8 describe Britain? Do you think one of the descriptions is more reliable than the other? Explain your answer.
3. Write a report describing the Roman invasion of Britain. Include the correct dates and the names of the different tribes and people involved in the invasion.

Challenge

Work in groups. Find out about the countries that the Romans conquered. Write a list of all these countries. Write the reasons why the Romans invaded different places. Write a list of the tribes they defeated in each place.

1.3 Roman settlers

There were 50 000 Roman soldiers in Britain – about 15 per cent of the whole Roman army. The soldiers lived in forts. The forts were spaced with one day's march between them. Between the forts, the Romans built roads so they could travel quickly across the country. How did Britain become more peaceful? What impact did the Romans make on Britain? What was it like in Roman Britain?

The Celts are defeated

Some Celtic tribes made peace with the Romans immediately. They agreed to obey Roman laws and pay taxes. Other tribes fought against the Romans and were defeated many times. Many tribes refused to join together with other tribes to make themselves stronger. So the Romans were able to attack individual tribes and beat them one by one. Over time, the country became more peaceful as the Romans defeated more and more tribes and made peace with other tribes.

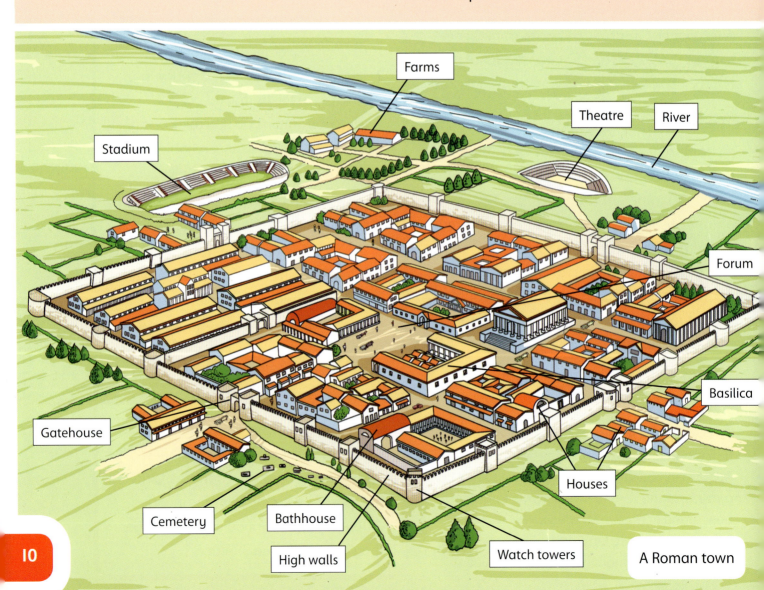

A Roman town

30/9/19

Glossary words

aqueduct   forum
basilica   tax
culture

The Romans build towns

The Romans built towns in every country they conquered. Roman towns were all laid out in the same way. They were protected by tall, thick walls and had straight streets laid out in a grid pattern. There were houses, shops, markets, meeting places, workshops, offices and temples.

The Romans tried to make their towns as healthy as possible. Pipes and aqueducts brought fresh, clean water from rivers and lakes. Drains carried away dirty water. Most towns had at least one bathhouse where people could go to wash, take exercise and meet friends.

Roman Britain

Over time, many tribes who lived far away from the Roman towns moved to be near the towns. They felt safer near the towns. The towns were built on flat land that was good for farming. Farmers sold crops and cattle to the Romans. There was plenty of work for people, either on the farms or building houses and roads for the Romans. Local rulers who supported the Romans prospered. They made money by trading in wool, gold, silver, lead and pottery. They often adopted Roman customs and dress. Slowly, the British and Roman cultures began to mix. The British people began to live like the Romans and the Romans adopted local traditions.

Did you know?

The Romans built excellent roads. They built their roads as straight as possible so that soldiers and goods could move quickly from place to place.

Activities

1. Write the answers to these questions.
   a. Why do you think some British tribes made peace with the Romans immediately?
   b. Why do you think other tribes continued to fight the Romans?
   c. Why did some tribes of Celts move to be near to the Roman towns?
2. Write a travel guide for someone visiting the town shown on page 10. Explain what the visitor can see and do.

Challenge

The Romans built aqueducts to bring fresh water into towns from a river or lake. The Romans built aqueducts in many of the countries they conquered. Some of these aqueducts still survive today. Find out about the nearest surviving aqueduct to the place where you live. Write a brief fact file about it and include some images.

1.4 Life in the Roman army

The strength of the Roman army was one of the main reasons why the Roman Empire became so large and powerful. It was the largest army in the world at this time. Roman soldiers were highly trained, well organised and had the best weapons and equipment. Who was in the Roman army? What uniforms did the soldiers wear? What was their training like?

Who could be a soldier?

Only men were allowed in the Roman army. There were two main types of Roman soldiers: legionaries and auxiliaries.

The best soldiers were called legionaries. A legionary had to be a Roman citizen, which meant he had to own property or farms. A legionary had to be tall, fit, literate and over 17 years of age. Legionaries stayed in the army for at least 20 years.

> 'The emperor was the first to give them more money and permission to wear gold rings and to live with their wives. This was in 197 CE.'

This was written by Herodian, a writer in Roman times. Before 197 CE, only the most important leaders in the army were allowed to marry.

Glossary words

armour	literate
auxiliary	pension
legionary	

The other type of soldier was called an auxiliary. An auxiliary was not a Roman citizen. Auxiliaries were recruited from tribes that had been conquered by the Romans. An auxiliary was not paid as much as a legionary and had to serve in the army for at least 25 years. Auxiliaries did many of the most dangerous jobs. For example, when the Roman army went into battle, auxiliaries fought in the front lines.

What uniforms did the soldiers wear?

A Roman soldier's uniform and equipment were designed to protect his body and help him to survive for long periods of time on military campaigns.

Did you know?

After a legionary had completed 20 years in the army he was allowed to retire. Retired legionaries received a pension or a large area of land. Some retired soldiers lived together in towns called colonia.

Fitness and fighting

Roman soldiers were very fit. They could march 32 kilometres in five hours, wearing all their armour and carrying their weapons and equipment. They practised sword-fighting and javelin-throwing every day. The soldiers could all cook, swim, sail boats and build bridges. Discipline was very strict in the Roman army. Soldiers could be executed if they failed to follow orders.

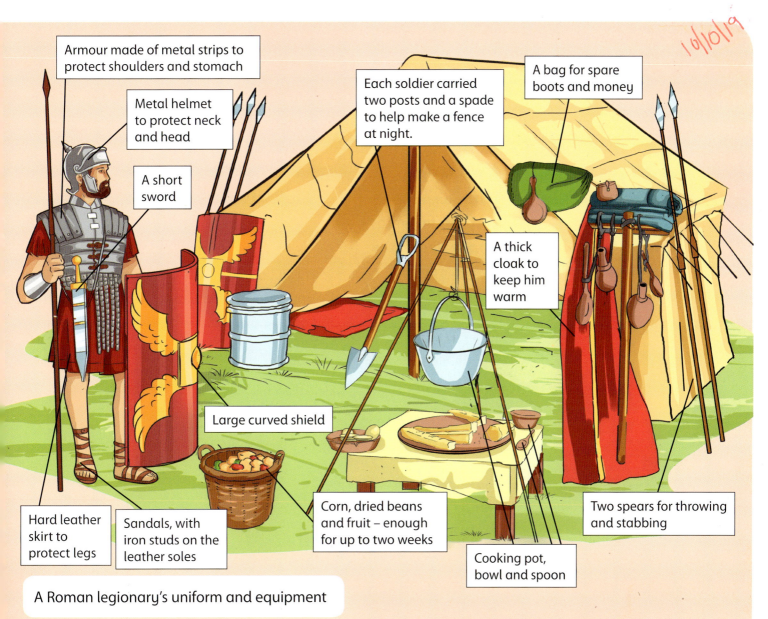

A Roman legionary's uniform and equipment

Activities

1. Write a list of three weapons or pieces of equipment that a Roman soldier carried. Explain how he used them.
   a. Why do you think the Roman army was so well trained?
   b. What might a Roman soldier do when he retired?
2. Design an advert to encourage men to join the Roman army. What sort of people do you want to attract? What should they be like? What sort of people should avoid joining the army?

Challenge

Different parts of the Roman army went into battle carrying Roman standards. Find out what a Roman standard was, what it looked like and why it was important.

1.5 What was a Roman villa like?

Look at the picture and photos. The picture on this page shows how a Roman villa might have looked. The photos on page 15 show the remains of two of the many villas built all over the Roman Empire during the Roman occupation. What was a Roman villa? Who lived in villas? What was it like to live in a villa?

Glossary words

archeologist · occupation · the past

What was a villa?

'Villa' is a Latin word. It means a large house in the country surrounded by its own grounds and other buildings.

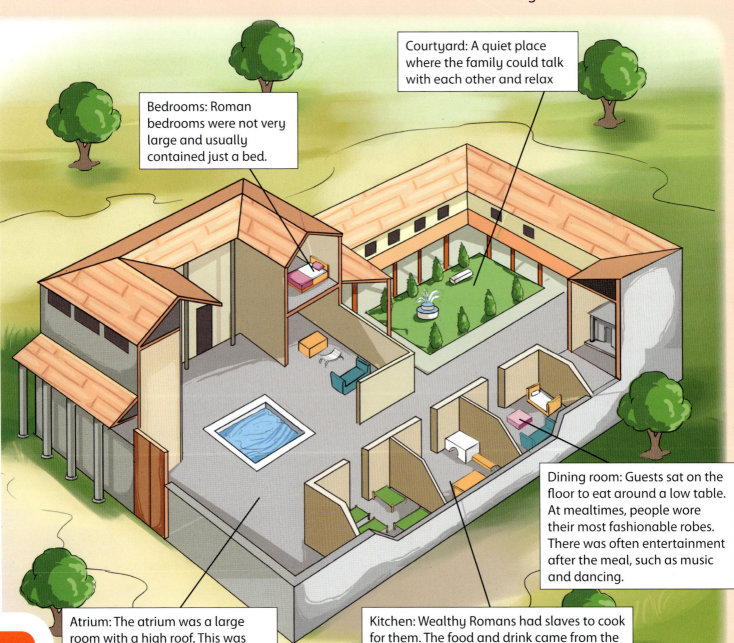

Courtyard: A quiet place where the family could talk with each other and relax

Bedrooms: Roman bedrooms were not very large and usually contained just a bed.

Dining room: Guests sat on the floor to eat around a low table. At mealtimes, people wore their most fashionable robes. There was often entertainment after the meal, such as music and dancing.

Atrium: The atrium was a large room with a high roof. This was where the owner of the villa greeted guests when they arrived.

Kitchen: Wealthy Romans had slaves to cook for them. The food and drink came from the local area and from all over the Roman Empire, if it was not available locally.

HYPOCAUST
An ancient roman heating system, comprising of a hollow space under the floor of a building into which hot air was directed.

Most villas had under-floor heating. The floor was raised up by pillars of stone or bricks and a small fire was lit to allow warm air to circulate.

HYPOCAUST?

Who lived in villas?

As the countries in the Roman Empire became more peaceful under Roman rule, some important and wealthy Romans decided to move out of the towns and build villas nearby. Soon there were hundreds of villas all over the Roman Empire, surrounded by farmland and workshops for iron-making and pottery. The villas were luxurious. The owners lived in the main building of a villa and the slaves and farm workers, who helped run the estate, lived in one of the smaller buildings.

Be a good historian

Good historians know that archeology is very important to help us understand the past. Archeology is the study of things that people made, used and left behind. The aim of archeology is to understand what people of the past were like and how they lived. People who study archeology are called archeologists.

Villas were decorated with beautiful wall paintings and mosaics like this one.

Activities

1. Imagine you are an estate agent in Roman times. Design a brochure or advert to sell the villa shown in the large picture.
2. In a group, write and perform a role play. One or two of you are the estate agents, showing buyers around a villa for the first time. The rest of the group are the buyers. The buyers should ask lots of questions about the property to test the estate agent's knowledge.

Challenge

Villas were built by the wealthier Romans outside the main towns. Most people lived in smaller houses or apartments in towns. Find out about the different types of home inside Roman towns. What did they look like? How many rooms did they have? How big were they?

1.6 The end of the Roman Empire

The Roman Empire grew for several hundred years. At the peak of their power, the Romans ruled between 50 and 90 million people across Europe, North Africa and the Middle East. The Roman army was the most powerful in the world and Rome had grown from a small town into an enormous and wealthy capital city. What happened to the Roman Empire? When and why did it decline?

A slow decline

The Roman Empire continued to grow until the time of Emperor Hadrian (117–138 CE). Hadrian decided the empire was too big to rule properly. He thought there was too much land for the Roman governors and the army to control and manage. From this time, the Roman Empire began to decline. The decline happened over a long period of time. Here are some of the reasons why the Roman Empire began to fail.

The empire is attacked

Many tribes from northern and central Europe attacked towns in the empire. The Romans called these people barbarians because the Romans thought they were uncivilised. There were so many attacks that the Roman army could not defend all the towns.

Poor leadership

The emperors were not always chosen because they were the best leaders. They sometimes bribed people to get the job. There were many arguments between important Romans. From 192 CE to 313 CE the Romans had over 40 different emperors. Many were assassinated.

Money

The empire was running out of money. Some emperors had wasted money on expensive parties and building projects. The Roman leaders had to raise taxes to pay for the army. This caused many people to rebel.

Did you know?

Britain was part of the Western Roman Empire. For many years, tribes attacked Britain. At first, more Roman soldiers were sent to defend Britain but eventually, in 410 CE, the Romans left. The Roman soldiers and leaders who ruled Britain were needed to defend other parts of the empire.

The empire was too big

The empire became so large it was difficult to control. In 285 CE, the Emperor Diocletian divided the empire into two parts, the Eastern Roman Empire and the Western Roman Empire. He believed that the empire would be easier to control if there were two emperors ruling separate parts of the empire. The Western part had its capital in Rome, the Eastern part had Byzantium as its capital (now Istanbul). There were many disagreements and wars because of this split.

The Roman army became weaker

As the empire grew, it needed more soldiers. There were not enough Romans to join the army, so more non-Romans were recruited. Many of these new soldiers were from the tribes in countries that the Romans had conquered – Gauls from France, Goths from Germany and Thracians from south-east Europe. These soldiers were not committed to the empire and did not always follow instructions properly in battle.

The fall of Rome

In 410 CE, a tribe of Goths attacked Rome (in the western part of the empire). They killed many Romans, destroyed buildings and stole treasures. In 476 CE, a tribal leader named Odoacer took control of Rome. He forced the last emperor of the Western Roman Empire (Romulus Augustulus) to step down as leader. This was the end of the Western Roman Empire. The Eastern Roman Empire continued for hundreds more years, but gradually got smaller and smaller.

Glossary words

assassinate	governor
barbarians	rebel

Be a good historian

Good historians know that there is rarely only one reason why something happens: there are often a number of different reasons. You might think some reasons are more important than others. A good historian always explains and justifies their ideas.

Activities

1. Work in a group. Discuss each of the reasons why the Roman Empire declined. Which do you think were the most important factors in the fall of the Roman Empire? Put the factors in order of most important to least important. Explain your choice of order in a class discussion.

2. Imagine you are a history expert on television. You have one minute to explain the decline of the Roman Empire. Write what you will say.

Challenge

Find out about the Eastern Roman Empire. Make a list of the countries in this part of the empire. Find out how it was ruled. Explain when and why this part of the empire declined.

1 Review

Answer these questions in your notebook.

Choose the best answer from the choices below. Write a, b or c as your answer.

1. The very best soldiers in the Roman army were the:
   a auxiliaries
   b legionaries
   c frontiers
2. To protect themselves in battle, Roman soldiers wore:
   a colonia
   b pensions
   c armour
3. In the Roman army, how many soldiers made up a century?
   a 60
   b 80
   c 100
4. The Romans held their shields together to protect themselves in battle. This action was called:
   a testudo
   b ronaldo
   c aqueduct
5. For how long did a legionary have to serve in the Roman army?
   a 20 years
   b 25 years
   c 30 years
6. Soldiers who fought on horses were called:
   a infantry
   b cavalry
   c century
7. In 60 CE, which Celtic warrior queen gathered a huge army and fought against the Romans?
   a Hadrian
   b Caledonia
   c Boudicca
8. Which Roman emperor divided the Roman Empire into two halves?
   a Julius Caesar
   b Romulus Augustulus
   c Diocletian

Decide if these statements are true or false. Write 'True' or 'False' for each one.

9. At the time of the Romans, Britain was ruled by tribes of people known as Celts.
10. The wall built across Britain to stop attacks from the north was called Caesar's Wall.
11. Aqueducts brought fresh water from rivers and lakes into Roman towns.
12. Roman villas had a large room with a high roof where the owners greeted guests. This room was called the courtyard.

Now complete these tasks.

13 Use the map to write a detailed description of when the Roman Empire grew and declined. Write a list of reasons why the Roman Empire declined and write a sentence to explain each reason.

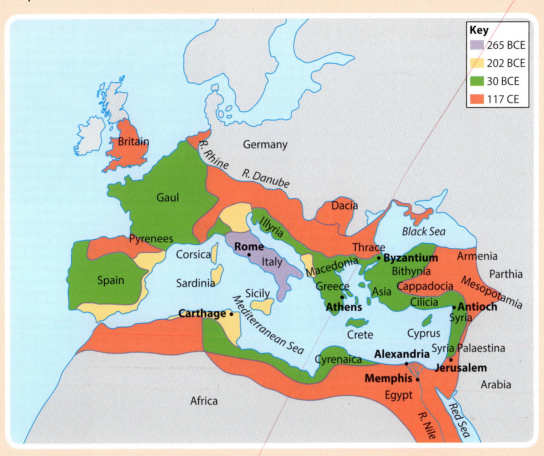

14 Name these three weapons and write a brief description of how the Roman army used each one.

a   b   c

15 Think about all the work you have done on the Romans and the Roman Empire. Do you think that the Roman invasions of other countries were always negative for the invaded countries? Or do you think that some countries may have welcomed the Romans?

2 The Anglo-Saxons

In this unit you will:
- explain who the Anglo-Saxons were
- explain who ruled the Anglo-Saxons
- describe what life was like in an Anglo-Saxon village
- recall achievements that the Anglo-Saxons are known for
- outline how the Anglo-Saxons and the Vikings are linked

? Look at the map. What does the map tell you about the Anglo-Saxon takeover of Britain?

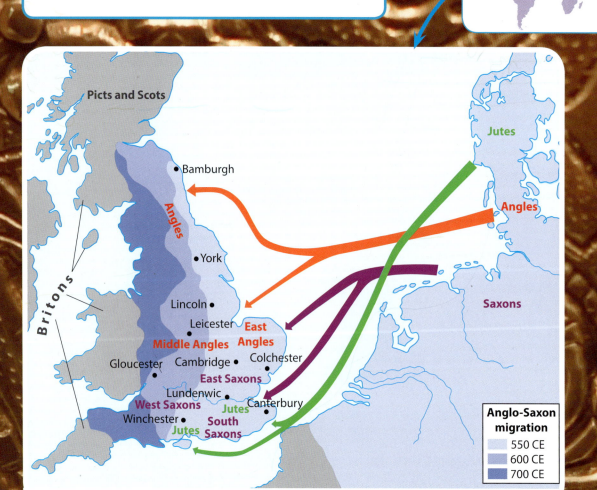

This map shows where the various Anglo-Saxon tribes came from and how they gradually took over Britain.

In about 410 CE, the Romans left Britain. They went back to Italy to defend parts of the Roman Empire nearer Rome. The British people no longer had the Roman army to defend them from invaders. It did not take long for new tribes to **invade** Britain. These tribes became known as Anglo-Saxons.

invade conquer
raid settle
kingdom

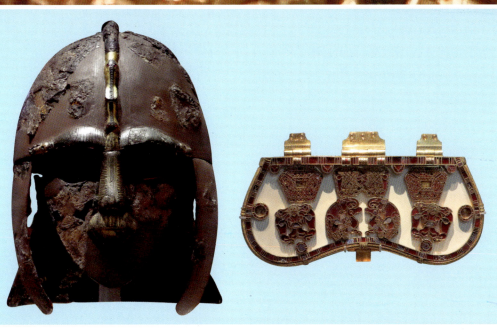

This helmet and decorated purse were among many Anglo-Saxon objects found buried in a field about 80 years ago at Sutton Hoo in Suffolk, England. The objects included a boat that was 27 metres long and nearly 5 metres wide.

The Romans
c500 BCE–476 CE

The (height of the) Maya
c250 CE–900 CE

The Anglo-Saxons
c400 CE–1066 CE

500 BCE

1100 BCE

2 The Anglo-Saxons

21

2.1 Who were the Anglo-Saxons?

The Anglo-Saxons were a mix of tribes from northern Germany, Denmark and the Netherlands. They crossed to Britain in large rowing boats. After the Romans left Britain, the Anglo-Saxons started to arrive. Some Anglo-Saxons immediately lived peacefully, but most fought with the British (known as Britons) for the land. When the Anglo-Saxons captured the land (which they usually did) they brought their families from their homeland. Who were the Anglo-Saxon tribes? Why did the Anglo-Saxons invade and settle?

Who were the Anglo-Saxons?

The Anglo-Saxons were a mix of three main tribes from northern Europe – the Angles, the Saxons and the Jutes. The Angles and the Saxons were the largest of the three attacking tribes, so we call them Anglo-Saxons. From 360 CE, even before the Romans left Britain, Anglo-Saxons **raided** the coast of Britain. They attacked villages and Roman villas and tried to steal gold, jewellery and animals. The Romans usually beat the Anglo-Saxons away quickly. When the Romans eventually left Britain, the Anglo-Saxons did not just raid the country and then return across the sea to their homelands. The Anglo-Saxons decided to **settle** in Britain instead.

An Anglo-Saxon warrior

The Anglo-Saxons were fierce warriors. Each soldier was armed with a battle-axe, a sword and a spear. The soldier carried a round shield and wore a metal helmet and a type of body armour called chain mail.

Glossary word

chain mail

Some Anglo-Saxons settled in Britain to find new farmland.

Did you know?

The Anglo-Saxons never conquered the whole of Britain. They never conquered Scotland, Wales or Cornwall.

Why did the Anglo-Saxons decide to settle?

There are two reasons why the Anglo-Saxons decided to settle in Britain.

Many Anglo-Saxons wanted to find new farmland. The climate was better in Britain. Also, their homelands often flooded, so it was difficult to grow crops.

Tribes of Picts and Scots attacked from the north (we call this Scotland today). Other British tribes invited the Anglo-Saxons to Britain to help defend homes and farms against the Picts and the Scots. The Anglo-Saxons did not leave: they settled in Britain instead.

Where did the Anglo-Saxons settle?

There were many battles between Anglo-Saxons and Britons. Over time, the Anglo-Saxons took control of most of Britain (see the map on page 20). Some of the Britons who were defeated in battle became the slaves of the Anglo-Saxons. Sometimes the Britons and the Anglo-Saxons settled down together and lived peacefully.

Be a good historian

Good historians know that there is usually more than one reason why something happens. There was more than one reason why the Anglo-Saxons invaded Britain.

Some Anglo-Saxons settled in Britain to help fight the Picts and Scots.

Activities

1   Create a diagram or poster that explains:
    a   who the Anglo-Saxons were
    b   why they travelled to Britain
    c   when they arrived in Britain
    d   how they **conquered** Britain
    e   where they settled.

    Your diagram or poster can contain no more than 100 words.

2   a   Explain the difference between 'raiding' and 'settling'.
    b   Were the Anglo-Saxons 'raiders' or 'settlers'?

Challenge

When the Anglo-Saxons defeated the Britons in battle, some Britons left the country. Find out where they went.

2.2 Who ruled the Anglo-Saxons?

The Anglo-Saxons did not have a single leader or emperor. There were many Anglo-Saxon tribes and each tribe had its own leader. Each tribe controlled a different part of Britain. The strongest and most successful tribal leaders were known as cyning. This was the Anglo-Saxon word for king. Each tribal 'king' ruled over a kingdom. Where were the main Anglo-Saxon kingdoms? How did a king rule his tribe? What different roles did people have in an Anglo-Saxon tribe?

Glossary word

witan

The king lived in a large wooden house, called a hall, where he held meetings. The king lived with his family and some of his most loyal warriors. Every farmer on the king's land gave him a share of the food they grew. The king also took land and treasures from other kings if he beat them in battle. Kings wore fine clothes, jewels and a crown.

Anglo-Saxon kings

Anglo-Saxon tribes were often at war with each other. They attacked each other because they wanted to gain more wealth and take valuable farmland. Sometimes a king who had conquered the land of several other kings called himself 'bretwalda', which meant 'ruler of Britain'.

Anglo-Saxon kingdoms

By about 600 CE, there were five main Anglo-Saxon **kingdoms**. Each kingdom had its own ruler. The map shows all these kingdoms.

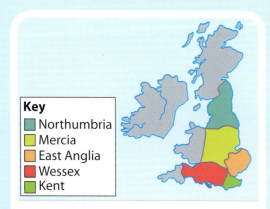

Key
- Northumbria
- Mercia
- East Anglia
- Wessex
- Kent

The main Anglo-Saxon kingdoms

Ordinary Anglo-Saxon villagers were called ceorls (pronounced 'churls'). They were farmers and skilled craftsmen, such as cloth-weavers, pottery-makers or metal-workers. They lived in small, wooden huts. Ceorls had to fight for their king in return for the land he allowed them to live on.

Some slaves were captured in battles with other tribes. Other slaves were criminals or were born into slave families. Slaves wore poor-quality clothes and were forced to work for their whole life. They slept in a barn with the animals.

Ruling a kingdom

If you were an Anglo-Saxon leader or king, life was difficult. People expected you to lead warriors in battle and protect your tribe's land from your rivals. Sometimes people in your kingdom tried to kill you because they wanted your power and riches.

Did you know?

Each king had a council of advisors to help him. This council of advisors was called the witan.

The thanes were the king's advisors. They travelled around the kingdom with the king and helped him to rule his people and organise his soldiers. The thanes owned large halls in the villages. They stayed in these halls when they visited the villages. They made sure that the villagers followed the king's laws. The thanes owned expensive jewellery and wore fine clothes.

Women had different roles from men. A king or thane's wife stayed at home, weaving cloth, sewing and looking after the children. Poorer women worked on the farms with the men. They also cooked, cared for children and made clothes.

Activities

1. Write one or two sentences to define an Anglo-Saxon kingdom.

2. Imagine you are an Anglo-Saxon king and a foreign king has come to visit you. Write a short speech explaining:

   a how Britain is divided

   b how an Anglo-Saxon king rules and controls his kingdom

   c which types of people the visitor will see in an Anglo-Saxon kingdom.

Challenge

Anglo-Saxons were often buried with their possessions. When archeologists discover Anglo-Saxon graves, they find evidence of the different jobs that men and women did and the skills they had. Read more about what was found buried at Sutton Hoo (there are some examples on page 21) and find out who may have owned these treasures.

2.3a What was life like in an Anglo-Saxon village?

The Anglo-Saxons built their own villages. They did not live in the stone houses and towns left by the Romans. They looked for land that was good for farming and near to a water supply, such as a river. Sometimes they cleared an area of forest to build their homes and farms. They used the wood from trees to build huts and fences to protect their cattle from wild animals such as wolves and foxes. They hoped the fences would also protect them from enemy attack. What was life like in an Anglo-Saxon village? How big were the villages? What was it like inside people's homes?

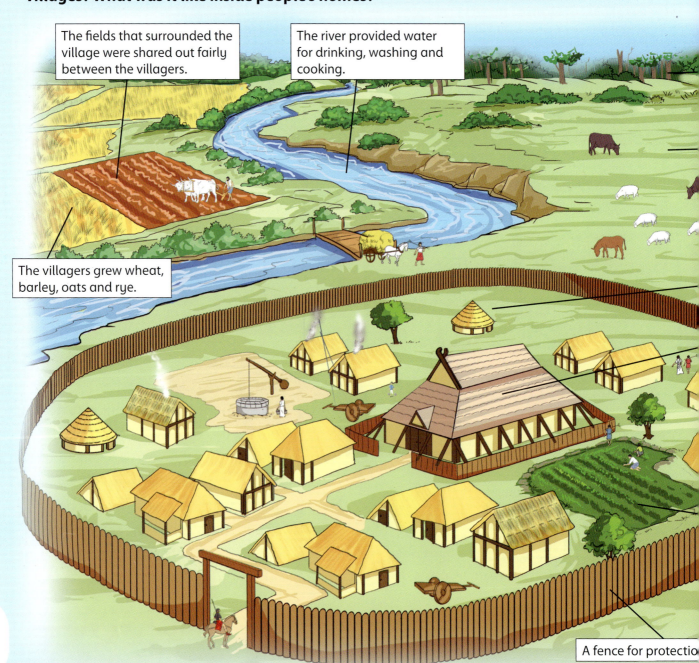

The fields that surrounded the village were shared out fairly between the villagers.

The river provided water for drinking, washing and cooking.

The villagers grew wheat, barley, oats and rye.

A fence for protection

Did you know?

The Anglo-Saxons gave England its name. 'Angle-land' (which later became England) means 'land of the Angles'. Scotland was also named after a tribe – the Scotti tribe.

Owning land

Most Anglo-Saxons were farmers. The ordinary villagers (called ceorls) owned enough land to grow their own food and keep some animals. They had some land next to their homes to grow vegetables and more land in some of the large fields that surrounded the village.

Glossary words

ceorl   thane

Homes and halls

The villages varied in size. Some contained just a few houses, but others had as many as 50 homes. The king's chief advisor (called a thane) lived in the largest house, which was called a hall. Thanes had slaves who farmed their land for them. The king owned a hall in some of the larger villages. He travelled from one village to the next. The villagers had to provide him with food.

- Wood for building homes and fences. People also burned wood to heat their homes.
- Farm animals provided meat, eggs, wool and milk. People used milk to make butter and cheese.
- A poor villager's or slave's hut
- The thane's hall
- An ordinary villager's home
- Villagers grew their own cabbages, onions, beans and herbs.

Activities

1. Imagine you travel back in time and meet someone who lived in the village pictured on these pages. What interview questions will you ask the person? How will you describe where you live to the person? What are the main differences between where you live and where the Anglo-Saxon lived? Are there any similarities?

2. Make a list of ways in which the Anglo-Saxons used their local environment and the resources around them.

Challenge

Life in an Anglo-Saxon village was wonderful if you were a king or a thane. Otherwise it was a very miserable life. Do you agree? Give reasons for your answer.

2.3b What was life like in an Anglo-Saxon village?

The homes of villagers in Anglo-Saxon times were very simple. They were made from wood and had roofs thatched with straw. Most houses had only one room. When it was very cold in winter, the villagers brought their animals inside the house. Look at the picture and read the information to discover what villagers' homes were like.

Glossary words

pottage   thatched

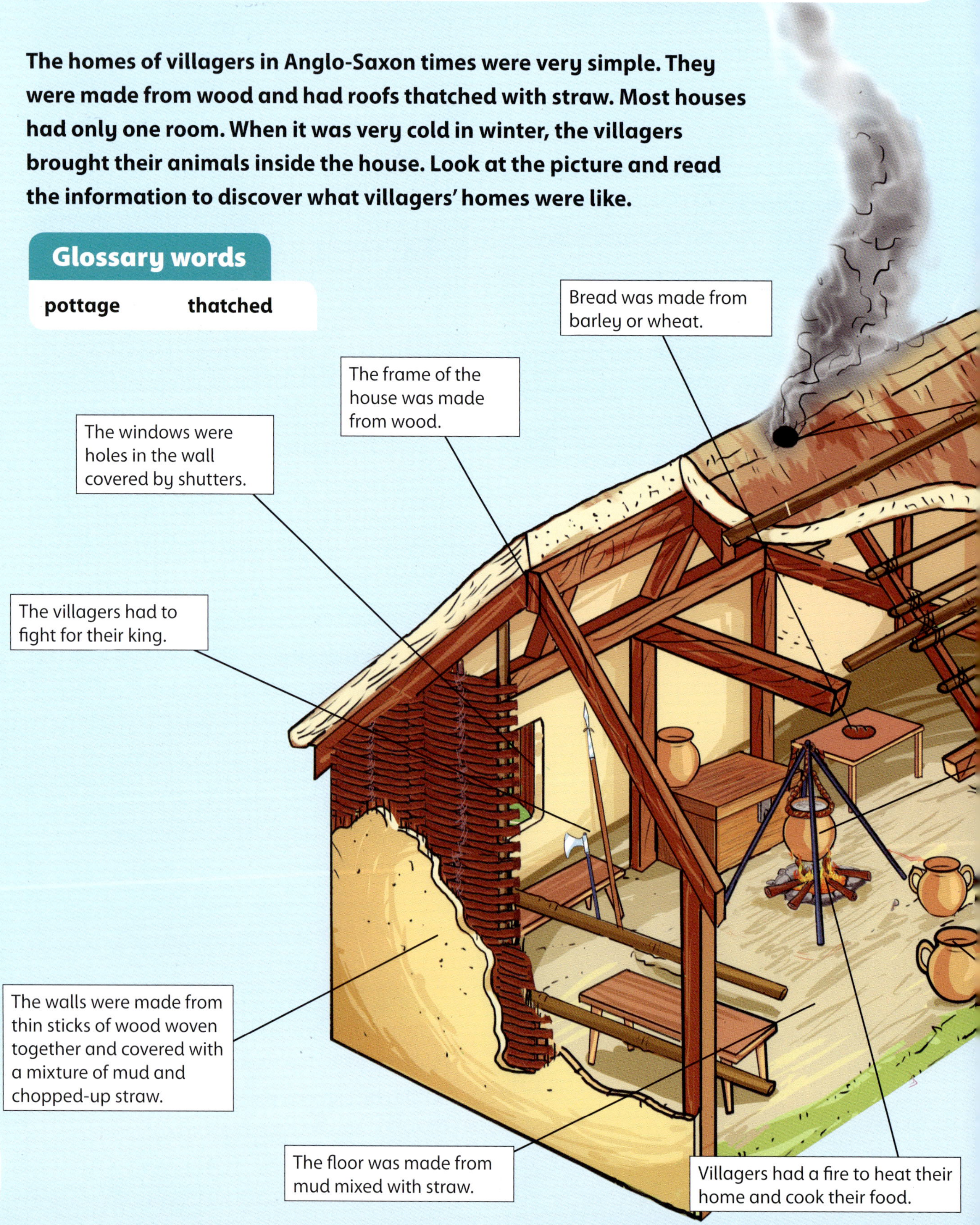

Bread was made from barley or wheat.

The frame of the house was made from wood.

The windows were holes in the wall covered by shutters.

The villagers had to fight for their king.

The walls were made from thin sticks of wood woven together and covered with a mixture of mud and chopped-up straw.

The floor was made from mud mixed with straw.

Villagers had a fire to heat their home and cook their food.

28

What about the children?

Ordinary Anglo-Saxon boys learned, from a very young age, all the skills they needed to be both a farmer and a warrior. They learned how to hunt and fish, plant crops and use swords, axes and spears. They had to behave like adults from about the age of 10. Like Anglo-Saxon women, girls had a different role from boys. Their mothers taught them how to cook, mend clothes, look after younger children and collect water and firewood.

Did you know?

The Romans lived in Britain before the Anglo-Saxons. The Romans built their homes with stone and had glass windows and under-floor heating. The Anglo-Saxons did not understand the Roman ways and did not like to live in the old, abandoned Roman towns. Sometimes, the Anglo-Saxons took some stone from old Roman towns and used it for their own buildings.

- A hole in the roof let the smoke out.
- Thatched straw roof
- People ate a thick soup called pottage every day. It contained vegetables such as peas, beans, onions and cabbages. Sometimes it also contained meat.
- Wood for the fire
- Villagers collected water for washing and cooking from a river or well.

Activities

1. Imagine you are an estate agent in Anglo-Saxon times. Design a brochure or advert to sell the house on this page.

2. Write a description of a day in the life of an Anglo-Saxon boy or girl. Think about the jobs the child does, as well as food, washing and sleeping. What are the main differences between your life today and the life of an Anglo-Saxon boy or girl? Are there any similarities?

Challenge

You have looked at an Anglo-Saxon village and an Anglo-Saxon house. These are from over 1000 years ago. Find out about a very old town or village near you or in a place you have visited. Who lived there long ago? How old is the town or village?

2.4 What were the achievements of the Anglo-Saxons?

When the Anglo-Saxons first began to settle in Britain, there were many different kingdoms that fought against each other. Over time, some kingdoms defeated others and took their land. By the 800s CE, there were three main Anglo-Saxon kingdoms: one in the north, one in the middle and one in the south. By now, Anglo-Saxon culture and society had become more advanced. What were the achievements of the Anglo-Saxons?

Making coins

When the Anglo-Saxons first came to Britain, they did not use coins. Most people used barter, which means that they exchanged goods. During the 8th century CE (the 700s), coins were used widely in Europe, for example in France. Soon, Anglo-Saxons began to produce their own coins to make trading easier. Coins with an image of the king showed how important and wealthy the king was.

An Anglo-Saxon coin from the time of Coenwulf, King of Mercia (796–821 CE). When this coin was sold in 2006 it was the most expensive coin ever purchased.

Anglo-Saxon crafts

The Anglo-Saxons were highly skilled craftspeople. Archeologists have found dice and board games made from bone, pottery, glass and stone. They have also found a musical instrument called a lyre (similar to a small harp). Anglo-Saxon metal-workers made iron tools, pots and swords. Wood-workers made wooden bowls, furniture, farming equipment and wheels.

Anglo-Saxon jewellers made beautiful belt buckles, brooches, necklaces, purses and ornaments. The jewellers used gold, silver, glass and precious stones from abroad. This shows that the Anglo-Saxons traded with other countries.

An Anglo-Saxon brooch

Writing

Educated Anglo-Saxons communicated with people in other European countries. For example, letters survive that were sent between Anglo-Saxon King Offa of Mercia and Emperor Charlemagne, who ruled over parts of France, Italy and Germany.

Glossary words

craftsperson   literature   trade

The Anglo-Saxons wrote books about the history of Britain. These books included pages that were beautifully and expertly decorated.

Part of a page from an Anglo-Saxon book

Poetry and storytelling

The Anglo-Saxons loved to create poems, songs and stories. They gathered together in halls to sing songs and hear poems such as *Beowulf*, the story of a heroic warrior who fights to save his people.

Buildings

At first the Anglo-Saxons avoided Roman towns and built their own villages instead, using wood. Over time, the Anglo-Saxons began to reuse the stone from Roman towns, villas and roads. Some Anglo-Saxon villages became important trading centres and began to grow. The Anglo-Saxons built ports on the south and east coasts of England. These quickly grew into busy centres of trade – local people and merchants bought and sold goods from all over Europe.

By 1000 CE, there were about 15 towns in Britain with more than 1000 people living in them. Eight of these towns had more than 3000 people living in them.

This Anglo-Saxon building from the 8th century CE was made from stone and still survives today.

Activities

1 How can a historian use the images on these pages to show that the Anglo-Saxons were highly skilled?

2 Work in a group to research other items of art and crafts, jewellery, coins and literature that provide information about Anglo-Saxon society and culture.

Challenge

In 2009, the largest ever collection of Anglo-Saxon gold and silver was found buried in a field in Staffordshire, England. Research the Staffordshire hoard. How many objects were found? How were they found? How much was the collection worth?

2.5 Viking invasions

From about 800 CE, 400 years after the Anglo-Saxons invaded Britain, the country was under attack from tribes from Denmark, Norway and Sweden. These tribes were made up of fierce fighters, usually known as Vikings but sometimes called Norsemen (meaning 'men from the north'). Why did the Vikings attack? How did they get to Britain? Did the Anglo-Saxons fight back?

Viking raids

The first recorded Viking attack on Britain was in 789 CE. This was the start of a long, violent struggle between the Anglo-Saxons and the Vikings. At first, the Vikings raided Britain. They travelled over the North Sea in longboats and stole valuable treasures, such as gold, jewels and books. They also took food, cattle, clothes and tools.

The Vikings could use their long, flat, narrow boats in both deep and shallow water. These boats could cross vast oceans and also travel close to the shore or along a river so Viking warriors could jump straight off the boats and fight.

Viking settlers

In 865 CE, an army of Vikings arrived in Britain. This time they wanted to conquer land and settle in Britain, not just raid the country and return to their homelands. The Vikings had many reasons for choosing Britain as a place to settle. Their land at home in Denmark, Norway and Sweden was not very good for growing crops or keeping animals. This meant that, as the population grew, there was not enough food. The Vikings were searching for better, more fertile land for their farms.

Glossary words

Danelaw   longboat

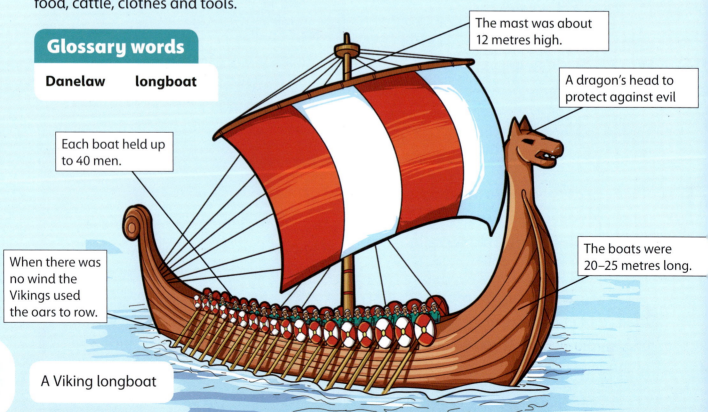

- The mast was about 12 metres high.
- A dragon's head to protect against evil
- Each boat held up to 40 men.
- The boats were 20–25 metres long.
- When there was no wind the Vikings used the oars to row.

A Viking longboat

During their raids, the Vikings had learned that Britain contained treasures that could make them rich.

The struggle for power

There were many battles between the Anglo-Saxons and the Vikings. Gradually, the Vikings conquered more and more land, taking control of most of the large Anglo-Saxon kingdoms. By 874 CE, only the Anglo-Saxon kingdom of Wessex in the south-west of England was not controlled by the Vikings. This area of England was ruled by King Alfred the Great. He beat the Vikings in battle but was unable to drive them completely out of the country.

Eventually, after many more years of fighting, King Alfred and the Vikings made a peace agreement. They decided to split the country into two – the Anglo-Saxon lands were in the west and the Viking lands were in the east. The area that the Vikings controlled was called the Danelaw.

At first the two sides continued to argue and fight, but gradually the Anglo-Saxons and Vikings became neighbours in Britain and there were many years of peace. By the mid-1000s CE, the country was united under one king, Edward. Edward's father had been an Anglo-Saxon king and his mother had once been married to a Viking king.

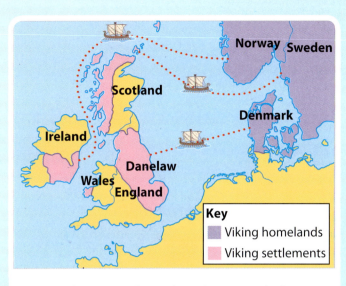

A map showing where the Vikings settled in Britain

Did you know?

The Vikings were great travellers and traders. They sailed all over Europe and the Atlantic Ocean in their longboats. The objects found at Sutton Hoo show that the Anglo-Saxons also traded with many distant lands. There were coins from France, bowls from Egypt, cloth from Syria and silver dishes from the Mediterranean.

Activities

1. Write a brief description of a Viking longboat.

2. Write a short paragraph explaining why the Vikings raided, and then settled, in Britain.

3. The Vikings raided and settled in many European countries. In a group, find out about these other raids and settlements. When were they? Where did the Vikings go? Why did they go to these places?

Challenge

The Anglo-Saxon age in Britain finally came to an end in 1066 CE when an army from Normandy in France invaded. Prepare a fact file about the events of the year 1066 and the new military force – the Normans – who came to rule England.

2 Review

Answer these questions in your notebook

Choose the best answer from the choices below. Write a, b or c as your answer.

1   The Anglo-Saxons came from:
    a   Germany, Denmark and the Netherlands
    b   Germany, Sweden and France
    c   Spain, Denmark and Germany
2   The Anglo-Saxons invaded and settled in Britain after the _____ left the country.
    a   Romans
    b   Vikings
    c   Celts
3   Most Anglo-Saxons were:
    a   shop owners
    b   sailors
    c   farmers
4   The roof of an Anglo-Saxon house was made from straw. It was called a _____ roof.
    a   hitched
    b   thatched
    c   wheat

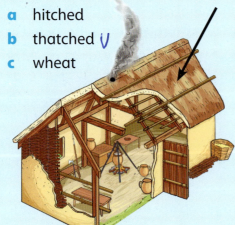

5   Ordinary Anglo-Saxon villagers ate a thick soup every day. It was called:
    a   village
    b   pottage
    c   cottage

6   Which of the following is a famous Anglo-Saxon poem?
    a   White wolf
    b   The tiger
    c   Beowulf
7   From about 800 CE, the Anglo-Saxons came under attack from:
    a   the Romans
    b   the Vikings
    c   the Celts

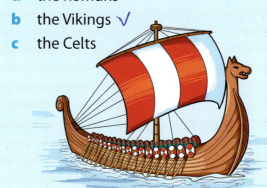

8   An ordinary Anglo-Saxon villager was called a:
    a   thane
    b   ceorl
    c   slave
9   When England was divided into two parts between the Anglo-Saxons and the Vikings, the name of the Viking area was:
    a   Viklaw
    b   Witan
    c   Danelaw

Decide if these statements are true or false. Write 'True' or 'False' for each one.

10 There were many Anglo-Saxon kings. Each king ruled over an area of land called a kingdom.
11 Anglo-Saxons were often buried with their possessions.
12 When the Anglo-Saxons first came to Britain, they brought coins with them.

Now complete these tasks.

13 Describe each of the people (1 to 5) in the pictures. Write their title (for example, king) and their role or job in Anglo-Saxon society. Finally, put them in order of importance in Anglo-Saxon society.

14 Compare the home of an ordinary Anglo-Saxon to the home you live in today. What are the main similarities and differences?

15 Create a timeline that shows some of the key dates and events in the history of the Anglo-Saxon period.

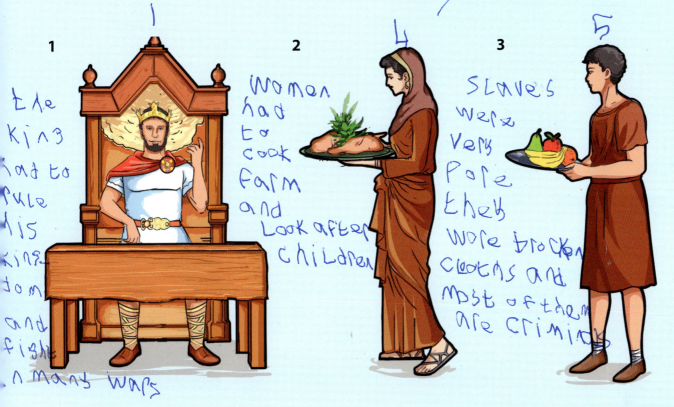

1 — 1 — the king had to rule his kingdom and fight many wars

2 — 4 — women had to cook farm and look after children

3 — 5 — slaves were very poor they wore broken clothes and most of them are criminals

4 — 3 — ceorls are skilled craftsmen and skilled farmers

5 — 2 — the thanes are the kings fight hand man and they order the troops

✓✓ super :)

3 The Maya

In this unit you will:
- explain why the Maya settled in the jungle
- recall who ruled the Maya
- explain what Mayan cities were like
- examine what achievements the Maya are known for
- explore what happened to the Maya

Key
- Coastal city-state
- Lowland city-state
- Highland city-state
- Tropical city-state

The Maya made their home in Central America. The former Mayan region covers southern Mexico, Guatemala, Belize, the northern part of Honduras and some of El Salvador.

28.1.19

About 2300 years ago, tribes called the Maya settled in the jungles, mountains and coastal areas of southern Mexico and Central America. They were skilled farmers and builders who created many beautiful cities. These cities contained palaces, temples, pyramids and homes. The cities were connected with roads that ran through the jungles. Each city was a centre of learning and the Maya achieved much in writing, art and science.

civilisation
society   city-state

? The Maya **civilisation** began about 2300 years ago. Approximately what year was that? The civilisation was at its height from about 250 CE to about 900 CE. What other civilisations and topics have you studied from this period of time? 281 BC

The Romans
c500 BCE–476 CE

The (height of the) Maya
c250 CE–900 CE

The Anglo-Saxons
c400 CE–1066 CE

500 BCE   1100 BCE

3 The Maya

37

3.1 Who were the Maya?

The first Mayan tribes were hunter-gatherers. This means that they moved around from place to place gathering food (such as fruit, seeds and nuts) and hunting animals for meat. Gradually, the Maya learned how to grow crops such as corn (which they called maize), squash and beans. This changed how the Maya lived. Why and how did knowledge of growing crops change Mayan civilisation?

Farming techniques

The Maya learned how to clear large areas of jungle to create fields to grow crops. They used tools made from stone, bone and wood. When they had removed most of the trees, they set fire to the remaining plants. They used the ash from these fires as a fertiliser that added nutrients to the earth. The ash helped the Maya to grow crops successfully. The Maya dug canals through the fields so they could water their crops.

Where the land was very wet, the Maya built raised platforms on which they grew crops. In mountainous areas, they used stepped farming, which means that they built terraces up the hillside. The terraces stopped the soil slipping downhill and provided a firm, flat base for the crops to grow.

A wide variety of food

Maize was a very important food for the Maya. They made corn flour from maize and used it to make bread. The most common type of bread was very thick and flat, known as a tortilla. The Maya also made porridge from maize. Mayan farmers grew many other crops, including sweet potatoes, tomatoes, avocados and chilli peppers. The Maya kept bees for honey and grew cotton to make clothes. They caught fish in the rivers and hunted wild turkeys and deer. The Maya used cacao beans to make a bitter chocolate drink, sometimes spiced with chilli.

Stepped farming using terraces helped the Maya to farm in mountainous regions.

Did you know?

Water was important for growing crops and for drinking. Where water was hard to find, the Maya collected rainwater and stored it in tanks and reservoirs.

Glossary words

maize	stepped farming
nutrients	terrace
squash	tortilla

The Maya used a flat, stone table known as a metate to grind corn into flour. They used the flour to make bread.

Settling down

Once the Maya began to farm, groups of people were able to settle in villages. The Maya were successful farmers so there was plenty of food and the population in these villages began to grow. Over time, cities started to develop.

Be a good historian

Remember that historians and archeologists do not always know the answers to questions in history. For example, experts are not completely sure why the Maya eventually abandoned their rainforest cities. The experts carry out research and look for clues, but sometimes they have to make an 'educated guess'.

Activities

1. Show your understanding by defining these words. Then explain why each of these things was important to the Maya:
   a maize
   b stepped farming
   c metate.
2. Write a brief report explaining:
   a how the Maya farmed
   b what Mayan farmers grew
   c why the Maya changed from hunter-gatherers to settlers.

Challenge

The Maya are believed to be the first people to discover how to make chocolate. Find out about the history of chocolate. How did the Maya enjoy chocolate? How did it become the type of chocolate we enjoy today?

3 The Maya

3.2 What were Mayan cities like?

The Maya never had one emperor ruling over them or just one central capital city. Instead, there were many independent areas, each controlled by a different king. These were called city-states. The city-state was the total area ruled by a king. The king and his advisors and all the important buildings were located in the main city, usually close to the centre of the city-state. How many city-states were there? What were Mayan cities like? How were the cities set out?

Mayan civilisation

There were many different **city-states**, but all the Maya spoke the same language – Mayan. At least 6 million people still speak Mayan today. People in all the city-states worshipped in the same way and followed similar laws. They planned their cities in the same way, with all the important buildings in the centre and the ordinary homes and farms on the edges. All the Maya dressed in a similar way and shared the same calendar.

The people who managed the city used these buildings.

The pyramids had great importance in Mayan culture and beliefs. The Maya used the pyramids as tombs for dead kings and as places for public ceremonies.

This is a ball court. Ball games were very popular with the Maya. In the Mayan city of Chichen Itza, in Mexico, archeologists have found at least 12 ball courts.

The Maya used an observatory to watch the movements of the sun, moon and stars. This was very important to the Maya. They used the positions of the stars and planets to decide when to plant and harvest their crops and when to go to war with another city-state.

The farms were on the edge of the city.

There were more than 60 separate city-states. Some of the biggest, such as Tikal, were home to about 100 000 people.

Rival city-states

For many years, historians thought the Maya were peaceful. However, archeologists discovered wall paintings, statues and carvings that recorded wars between rival city-states. Sometimes one city-state became very powerful and gained control of some of the smaller city-states. But no state managed to control the whole Mayan civilisation.

Teotihuacan, a city of over 100 000 people, was a centre for trade. By 500 CE, it was the sixth largest city in the world. The larger pyramid shown here is the third largest in the world.

Did you know?

The Maya built their spectacular buildings without metal tools, the wheel or large animals (such as the donkey, ox or elephant) to help them.

Activities

1. Research one Mayan city-state and find images. Write a fact file about the city-state you have researched.
2. Create a travel guide for someone visiting the city-state. You can write your guide for someone visiting the city-state today, or for someone visiting long ago.

Challenge

The Maya were one of many civilisations of southern Mexico, Central America and South America. Use books and the Internet to research and prepare fact files about the Olmec, Inca and Aztec civilisations.

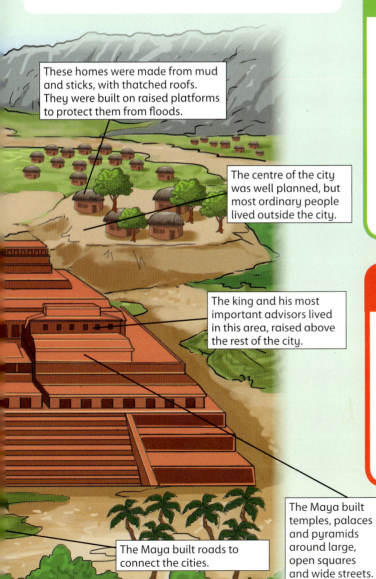

- These homes were made from mud and sticks, with thatched roofs. They were built on raised platforms to protect them from floods.
- The centre of the city was well planned, but most ordinary people lived outside the city.
- The king and his most important advisors lived in this area, raised above the rest of the city.
- The Maya built roads to connect the cities.
- The Maya built temples, palaces and pyramids around large, open squares and wide streets.

Glossary words

pyramid   tomb

41

3 The Maya

3.3 Who ruled the Maya?

Each Mayan city-state had its own king. When a king died, his son or other closest relative became the next king. Who helped the king rule? What were the different levels in Mayan society? How do we know so much about the Mayan kings?

The king and his family

Each city-state had a ruling family. The king, his wives and children were at the top of Mayan **society**. They lived a life of luxury in large palaces in the centre of the city. People believed that members of the royal family were more important than anyone else and thought the royal family could protect them. The king performed special ceremonies to protect his city and bring good fortune.

There was only one way for a new ruling family to take over a city-state. This happened when the ruling family in another city-state challenged and defeated the king's family. Fights and wars between city-states were common. In times of war, the king led his army into battle.

Helping the king

A group of men known as the nobles helped the king to rule. The nobles were generals and other officials. They were usually members of the king's family.

Mayan nobles spent a lot of time on their appearance. They wore brightly coloured clothes and painted their bodies. They wore lots of necklaces, hair bands, bangles and enormous earrings.

This painted pottery figure shows a Mayan noble.

They also wore huge hats – the taller the better! The hats were usually decorated with long feathers from the quetzal bird, which had tail feathers up to 1 metre long.

Some women played an important role in Mayan society. The wives and mothers of kings sometimes held positions of influence. At a lower level than the nobles were the craftspeople, architects and merchants. This group could become wealthy, but they were not allowed to become nobles, unless the king invited them. They could not even dress like a noble. At the next level were the farmers, who lived outside the city centre on their farms. At the lowest level were the slaves. Most slaves were captured in wars from other city-states. Some people became slaves as a punishment for a crime. Slaves did much of the building work and had no rights or privileges.

How do we know about Mayan people?

We know a lot about the rulers of the larger city-states because the Maya recorded the kings' reigns. Information about the kings was painted onto pottery or carved in wood or stone.

Glossary words

nobles
reign
record
social class

Crime and punishment

Laws were similar across all the city-states. If a person broke a law, a judge listened to the evidence and decided whether the person was guilty or not. The punishments varied. A thief might become a slave of the victim for a short while. The punishment for damaging someone else's property was to pay for the damage or become a slave. Murder was rare. The punishment for murder was execution or the family of the victim might decide to take the murderer's land instead.

Stone columns known as stelae were carved out of limestone. The stelae recorded the actions and achievements of the kings.

Activities

1. Create a diagram to show how Mayan society was organised. Remember to show and explain the differences between the various groups.
2. Write a description of the system of law and order in Mayan society. Carry out some extra research on crime and punishment.

Did you know?

The organisation of society was very strict. It was very difficult to move from a position within society. If a person's father was a farmer or a merchant, then that person became a farmer or a merchant. People could not marry outside their social class.

Challenge

Research and write a report about one of the Mayan kings. King Pakal of Palenque is one of the most famous kings. He became king when he was 12 years old. The rulers of the city-states were nearly always men, but there were sometimes queens. You could research the Lady of Tikal.

3.4 Mayan merchants

There were many city-states. Each city-state traded with others. The large trading network was very important for the city-states. Why was trading so important? What goods did the Maya trade? How did the merchants travel?

Why did the city-states trade?

The city-states had most – but not all – of the goods they needed. Each city-state had to trade with other city-states to get the goods it needed. Different city-states had different resources to trade.

- City-states near the coast had plenty of fish and salt. Salt was important for preserving food. But the coastal city-states had poor farmland so they traded their fish and salt for maize and other vegetables.
- Material for making tools and for building, such as flint and limestone, was available in the city-states in the lowland areas. The lowland city-states traded building materials for shrimp, lobsters and crabs from the coastal city-states or for valuable stones from the highlands. Jade and obsidian (a type of glass found in volcanic areas) were highly prized.
- The city-states in the tropical areas traded skins from jungle animals, feathers, wood and cacao beans for the goods they needed.

Jade or chocolate money

The Maya did not use coins or notes to buy and sell. The merchants agreed between themselves how much of their goods they would swap for something they wanted. This is called bartering. Sometimes merchants carried jade or cacao beans with them to swap for goods because these resources were so valuable.

Glossary words		
bartering	material	textiles

This jade jewellery set was found in the jungle city-state of Calakmul, Mexico, and is from 600–900 CE. Jade was popular in all the city-states.

Merchants

The people who travelled around the region trading goods were known as merchants. Merchants were well respected and many lived very comfortable lives. They did not use donkeys or elephants to help them transport goods. They used people from their own city-state or slaves. The city-states were linked by well-built roads. Sometimes the merchants used rivers or sailed in the sea, close to the shore so they did not get lost.

This picture shows a merchant and craftsmen trading stone axes and hammers. Can you also see the men carrying goods to the next city-state, the women putting maize into pots and the farmers in the fields?

The merchants also used canoes made from hollowed-out tree trunks. These boats were up to 15 metres long, 2.5 metres wide and powered by 25 rowers.

Activities

1. Write a report on trading between Mayan city-states. Include:
   a why trading was important for city-states
   b what is meant by 'bartering'
   c how merchants travelled between the city-states.
2. Write a description of the picture at the top of the page, giving as much detail as possible about the people you can see and what each person is doing.

Did you know?

Sometimes a merchant arrived in a city-state with a wide variety of goods to trade – fine pottery, stone axes, textiles, feathers, gold, jade, honey, animal skins, vegetable dyes, herbal medicines, bags of salt, paper (produced from fig-tree bark), jewellery and furniture.

Challenge

Feathers were important and valuable to the Maya. Feathers were one of the most popular items that Mayan merchants traded. Find out the different types of bird that were the source of the feathers. How did the Maya use the feathers?

3.5a What achievements are the Maya known for?

The Maya are well known for their great stone cities in the jungle and their huge pyramids. They were also very advanced in their use of mathematics and writing. The Maya studied the movements of the stars and planets and created an accurate calendar. What was Mayan writing like? Why were the Maya so interested in astronomy? What art did they create?

Great artists

The Maya were very artistic. They created beautiful vases and bowls out of clay and made jewellery and small statues in jade, stone, gold, silver, wood and bone. The Maya did not use metal tools. They used tools made from hard stone. They carved stelae (see page 43), which told stories of their kings, and they painted pictures on palace walls. Weavers created colourful fabrics using dyed cotton. The bright material was usually made into clothing, but it was sometimes used as wall hangings to decorate people's homes.

Mayan mathematics

Mayan mathematics was very advanced. Our number system is based on the number 10, but the Maya based their system on the number 20. It is believed that this was because humans have 20 fingers and toes. The Maya used just three symbols to show numbers: a dot (for '1'), a line (for '5') and a seashell (for zero). The Maya were one of the first groups of people to use the number zero. With their number system they could add and subtract, record large numbers and accurately keep track of dates.

Glossary words

codex   hieroglyphics   symbol

The number system of the Maya

Mayan writing

The Maya created a written language, known as hieroglyphics (or glyphs). The glyphs were pictures that represented words, sounds and objects. The Maya used glyphs to record important events and stories about their leaders. They carved the glyphs onto stone columns or the walls of stone buildings. They also created books using paper made from tree bark. A book was called a codex. The plural of codex is 'codices'.

sun   fire   cloud   woman

house   shield   blue/green   mountain

year   person   water   snake

A selection of glyphs. The Mayan writing system had about 700 glyphs.

Part of one of only four codices that have survived

Activities

1. Research Mayan works of art made from jade, clay, stone, gold, silver, wood and bone. Create a presentation to show and describe some of the works of art.

2. Design three new glyphs. Swap your glyphs with a friend. Can your friend work out what the glyphs mean? Discuss where we use images instead of words, sounds or objects in today's world.

Challenge

Carry out some detailed research into Mayan clothing. How did the different groups in Mayan society dress? How did the Maya make their clothes? What types of jewellery were popular? How else did the Maya decorate their bodies?

Did you know?

The land that the Maya occupied is made up of rainforests, mountains and coasts. The mountain areas are the highlands and the areas nearer to sea level are the lowlands.

3.5b What achievements are the Maya known for?

Serious sports

The Maya played a type of football called pok-a-tok. Two teams played against each other in a large ball court with sloping sides and areas for spectators. Without using hands, each team tried to keep a hard rubber ball in the air and get it through stone rings on the side of the court. People probably played pok-a-tok for fun, but some experts believe it was also a way of settling conflicts. They think that sometimes members of the losing team were executed.

The remains of a ball game court in the ancient city of Uxmal, Mexico

Studying the stars

The Maya were very interested in astronomy. They used observatories to watch the movements of the sun, planets and stars. They predicted eclipses and solstices. There are two solstices in the year: the longest day and the shortest day. The Maya used their observations to create three different calendars. They used one calendar to record all history over a long period of time and another calendar to plan special ceremonies. For farming, they used a calendar of 365 days, like the one we use today.

Archeologists think this building was an observatory used to study the night sky.

Did you know?

The Maya believed that crossed eyes were a sign of beauty. They dangled objects in front of a newborn baby's eyes, until the baby's eyes were completely (and permanently) crossed.

Glossary words

astronomy   observatory

The Maya used their knowledge of astronomy when planning their buildings. The pyramid at Chichen Itza has 365 steps. Some Mayan buildings have windows for viewing the movement of the planet Venus. Mayan generals believed that it was good luck to fight battles when Venus was in a certain position in the sky.

What happened to the Maya?

Mayan civilisation was at its peak from about 250 CE to 900 CE. However, after 900 CE the Maya abandoned many of the cities in the rainforests. Experts are not sure why this happened. Here are some theories:

- Some experts believe that the cities grew so big that they used up all the farmland. As a result, the cities could not grow enough food so there were many famines.
- Other experts think that there were so many violent wars between the city-states that some large groups of Maya were wiped out. Other Maya might have run away from the rainforests and moved to places where they felt safer.
- Some scientists think that there was a series of droughts and there was not enough water for the crops.

The rainforest cities were abandoned after 900 CE, but many other city-states continued for hundreds of years. Then, in about 1500 CE, Spanish invaders began to conquer the Mayan city-states. Many Maya died fighting against the Spanish. Others died because they caught diseases that the Spanish brought with them. Eventually, the Spanish conquered all the city-states. However, the descendants of the Maya continue to live in the area today.

Mayan women pictured recently in traditional coloured clothing. The Mayan people still make up the majority of the population in Guatemala, Central America.

Activities

1. Create a poster or a presentation called 'The achievements of the Maya'. Give examples of Mayan mathematics, writing and astronomy.
2. Create a newspaper article or television news report that explains different theories about what happened to the Maya. Carry out your own research to find out other theories.

Challenge

Find out about the Spanish invasion of Mayan land. When did the Spanish explorers arrive on Mayan land? Why did they go there? How did the Maya resist the invaders? How long did it take the Spanish to gain control?

3 Review

Answer these questions in your notebook.

Choose the best answer from the choices below. Write a, b or c as your answer.

1. A very important food for the Maya was:
   a. apples
   b. (maize) ✓
   c. cheese

2. In a Mayan city-state, all the palaces, temples and pyramids were:
   a. (in the centre of the city) ✓
   b. on the edge of the city
   c. near to the river

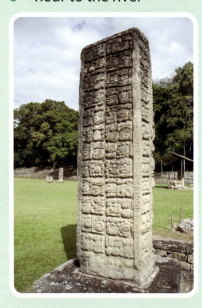

3. The Maya recorded the actions and achievements of their kings on carved stone columns. The columns are called:
   a. (stelae) ✓
   b. stables
   c. shinto

4. Exchanging goods without using money is called:
   a. transporting
   b. (bartering) ✓
   c. seasoning

5. A Mayan book is called a:
   a. glyph
   b. solstice
   c. (codex) ✓

super!

6. How many Mayan books are thought to exist today?
   a. (4) ✓   b. 8   c. 12

7. A popular Mayan ball game was:
   a. tic-tok
   b. (pok-a-tok) ✓
   c. ping-pong

8. A glyph is:
   a. an item of clothing
   b. a type of jewellery
   c. (a small image used to represent a word, sound or object) ✓

9. How many calendars did the Maya use?
   a. 1   b. 2   c. (3) ✓

Decide if these statements are true or false. Write 'True' or 'False' for each one.

10. The Maya used tools made from metal. F ✓
11. The Maya were one of the first groups of people to use the number zero. t ✓
12. The Maya used kidney beans to make a chocolate drink. F ✓

Now complete these tasks.

13 Describe how society in a Mayan city-state was organised, beginning with the king and ending with the slaves.

14 Look at the map. You can see four different areas where city-states were built: coastal areas, lowland areas, highland areas and tropical areas.
   a What resources did each of the four areas produce and trade.
   b Why was trade so important for the Mayan city-states in the different areas?

15 Compare a Mayan city to the town or city you live in today. What are the main similarities and differences?

Handwritten annotations:
- (Remember my pyramid).
- King, Nobles, Merchants, Slaves (only missed farmers)
- 21.5.19
- Coastal – fish
- Lowland – flint/limestone
- Highlands – Jade/valuables
- Tropical – Cacao beans, feathers etc.

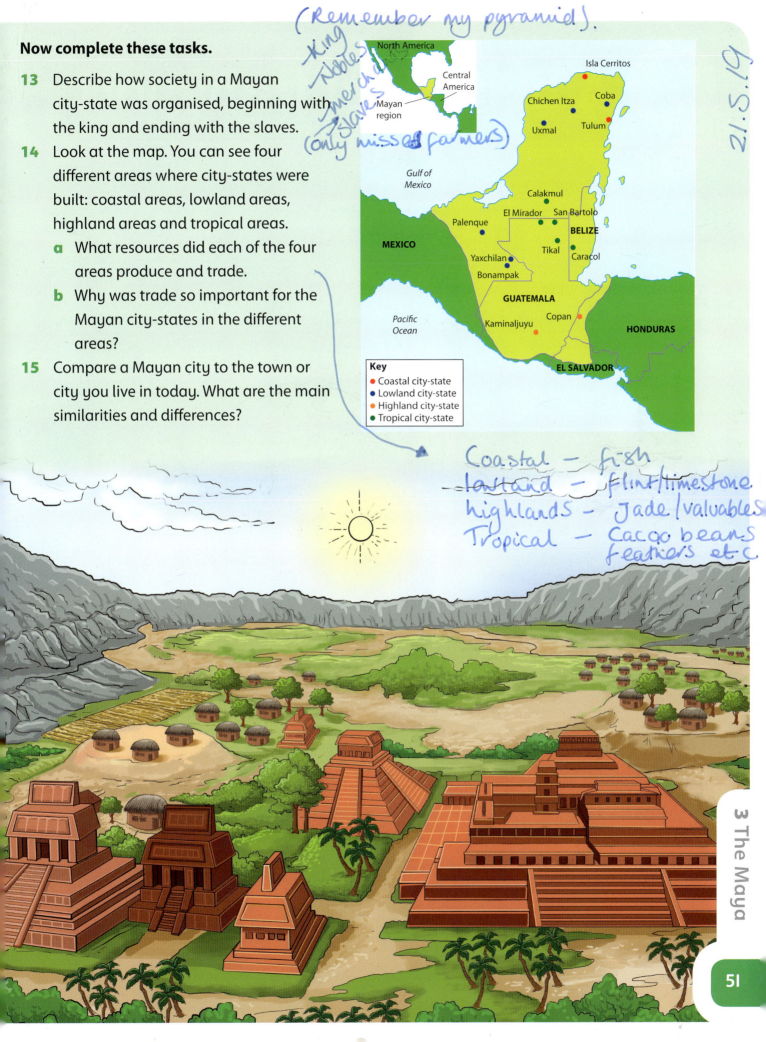

4 A history of transport

In this unit you will:
- explain why the invention of the wheel was so important
- discover what methods of transport were common before the wheel
- explore how transport and trade are linked
- explain the impact of technology on transport
- examine how developments in transport have changed people's lives

c8200–7600 BCE	c4000 BCE	c3000 BCE	468 BCE	1400–1700 CE	1783	1804
Oldest 'dugout' boat ever found dates from this time	Sails used on boats	Experts think the first wheel was invented about this time	Work began on the Grand Canal of China	The Age of Exploration	Montgolfier brothers created a hot air balloon that carried people	First steam locomoti

We use many different types of transport to move people and goods from one place to another. Today, high-speed trains, planes and cars are very common. Even the idea of humans travelling into space is quite normal. There were many **developments** in transport before humans could travel as we do today.

invention
development
technology

? Look at the photos of different methods of transport. Can you put the methods of transport in chronological order? Can you suggest any more methods of transport?

| 25 World's first passenger railway opened in Britain | 1869 Suez Canal opened | 1885 First motor car powered by an internal combustion engine | 1903 First engine-powered flight in an airplane | 1908 Ford began production of the Model T on an assembly line | 1961 Russian Yuri Gagarin became the first human in space |

4 A history of transport

53

4.1a On the road

The invention of the wheel changed how people travelled. The wheel made it much easier to transport people and goods further and faster. When was the wheel invented? How did people move heavy objects before the invention of the wheel? How has technology changed the way in which we use the wheel?

Heavy objects moved easily over rolling poles known as rollers.

Before the wheel

Before the **invention** of the wheel, people either walked everywhere or rode on an animal. Some people used a horse, camel or donkey to carry goods to market. When things were too heavy for a human or an animal to carry, people used rollers or a sledge. Sometimes a team of people worked together to carry a heavy load.

Using roads

The first roads linked villages and towns. People travelled along the roads to visit markets and to trade goods. The roads began as simple dirt tracks that people created by travelling to and from places along the same route. The roads often followed rivers or valleys.

The first roads were mainly used for trade and were called trade routes. Some of the earliest long-distance trade routes over land date from about 1500 BCE in Western Asia, the Mediterranean, China and India. Traders transported goods such as silk and spices from one place to another. Some of the best roads of the ancient world were built by the Romans. The Romans built a network of roads so the Roman army could march quickly from one part of the empire to another. Merchants also used these roads. By 300 CE, the road network of the Roman Empire reached from Italy to France, Britain and the eastern Mediterranean region.

Before the invention of the wheel, animals carried or pulled heavy goods to market.

Glossary word

trade route

Roman roads were so well built that some still survive today. Others have been renovated, using the same route as the Roman road.

The invention of the wheel

No-one knows who invented the wheel, but experts think that the first wheels were made about 5000 years ago. The oldest known wheel was from Mesopotamia, which is the name of an ancient region covering modern-day Iraq, Kuwait and the eastern parts of Syria. Some experts think that the Mesopotamian people invented the wheel – and news of the invention spread very quickly along trade routes. Other experts believe that the wheel developed in separate parts of the world at about the same time. The first wheels were made from wood. The wheel changed the way in which people travelled. People could travel much faster and large carts with wheels could carry heavy loads over long distances.

Challenge

Use the Internet and books to research the invention of the wheel. Where do experts think the wheel was invented? How did the wheel develop over time?

Did you know?

People in many countries have used strong animals, such as donkeys, camels and horses, for transport for thousands of years. However, the Maya did not use animals to transport the materials they needed to build their cities. Instead, they either used slaves or employed people from their own cities. The Maya did not use the wheel either.

Activities

1. Create a presentation or diagram to show how people travelled and transported goods before the invention of the wheel.

2. How and why did roads develop? First, explain where the first roads were located and what they were used for. Then explain why a network of roads developed.

3. Describe the impact of the invention of the wheel. Explain how the wheel changed the ways in which goods and people moved around.

Be a good historian

Good historians know that change can happen very quickly, but it can also happen very slowly. For example, for many thousands of years a cart or coach, pulled by an animal, was the quickest way to travel. The invention of rail, air and motor transport greatly increased the speed of travel.

4.1b On the road

As the world population grew, the number of towns and villages increased. As a result, the number of roads that linked these places also increased. Advances were made in bridge-building and road-making techniques, so the quality of roads in many countries slowly improved. However, most people still travelled around on foot or used strong animals to pull goods and people in coaches and carts.

Getting faster

There have been many different uses of the horse and cart all over the world. For example, armies used fast, light, two-wheeled chariots in battle and to transport soldiers quickly from one place to another. As roads continued to improve, horse-drawn coaches became a popular way to transport goods quickly. In Britain, the quickest way to transport goods was by stagecoach. A stagecoach was a large, light, horse-drawn coach that travelled regularly over a fixed route carrying passengers and goods.

A painting of a British stagecoach, about 1805

The first cars

The first car that could move using its own power was built in France in 1769. It was powered by a steam engine and could travel at about 7 kilometres per hour. In 1837, the first electric car was built. It was powered by batteries.

At this time, a new fuel was made from oil, called petrol. Inventors began to build engines that were powered by burning petrol. These new engines were called internal combustion engines.

Inventor Karl Benz with his assistant Josef Brecht in the 1885 Benz Motorwagen (motor car)

In 1885, a German man named Karl Benz decided to put one of the new engines on a three-wheeled vehicle he had made in Mannheim, Germany. This is known as the first motor car. It had a tiny engine at the back and could travel at about 12 kilometres per hour. It has the same type of engine we still have in most of our cars today.

Motor cars

Motor cars soon became more and more popular. Lots of companies all over the world began making cars – for example, Peugeot in France (1891), Fiat in Italy (1899), Dodge and Cadillac in the United States (1902), Rolls-Royce in Britain (1906) and Audi in Germany (1909).

These car manufacturers were later joined by BMW in Germany (1916), Toyota in Japan (1937), Ferrari in Italy (1939) and Hyundai in South Korea (1967).

Factories and cars

In 1908, Ford Motor Company in the United States began making one of the most famous cars ever made – the Model T. The Model T was the first car made in large numbers in a factory on an assembly line. The car was cheap and easy to drive. Over 15 million Model Ts were sold between 1908 and 1927, making it one of the best-selling cars in history. At the peak of production, Ford produced about 10 000 Model Ts every day. It was such a well-built car that some Model T cars still survive.

Today, most cars are made on an assembly line in the same way as the Model T.

The Ford Model T

Glossary words

assembly line   stagecoach
chariot   vehicle
environmentally friendly

Modern motors

In recent years, some cars have been criticised for the amount of pollution they put into the environment. Many car-makers have started to introduce more 'environmentally friendly' versions of their cars known as hybrids. Most hybrid cars have an electric motor for short journeys and a petrol engine for longer journeys.

Other motorised vehicles

Manufacturers also started fitting engines to carts and carriages. These vehicles eventually became the trucks, lorries, buses and coaches that transport goods and people on today's roads.

Activities

1. Use the information from this book and other research to write an article for a school newsletter that describes the history of the motor car.

2. Prepare a fact file on the history of the car industry in a country of your choice.

Challenge

Find out when rubber tyres and diesel engines were first used for cars. Also find out when and why windscreen wipers, air conditioning and car radios were first used in cars.

4.2 Water transport

From the earliest times, people have used boats to travel. They used boats to catch fish, trade goods and explore the places where they lived. How were the first boats made? How have different people used boats? How have boats changed over time?

The first boats

People have been travelling on water for tens of thousands of years. The first boats were simple rafts made from tree logs tied together, and dugout (canoes) made from hollowed-out tree trunks. The oldest boat ever found in the world is a dugout. It was made some time between 8200 and 7600 BC.

The oldest boat ever found. It was found in the Netherlands in 1955. It measures 298 centimetres long and 44 centimetres wide.

People in different parts of the world used different types of boat. A coracle is a light, round boat made by sewing animal skins over a wooden frame. Coracles were popular in India, Vietnam, Iraq and Tibet. In parts of the Middle East, northern Africa and South America, reed boats were common. Reeds are a type of long grass found near rivers.

Reed boats were made by tying reeds together. A 7000-year-old reed boat was found in Kuwait in 2002.

A reed boat

A coracle

Sail boats

Experts think that people began to use the power of the wind to push their boats over long distances about 6000 years ago in Mesopotamia (modern-day Iraq, Kuwait and the eastern parts of Syria). Sails were made from cloth or strips of thin wood. The sails were hung from a pole (called a mast) to catch the wind. Merchants used some of the earliest known sail boats on the Nile, Euphrates and Tigris rivers more than 5000 years ago.

Using boats for war

Boats have also been used in wars. The Romans and the Vikings, for example, used ships to transport soldiers and goods from one place to another. In the 14th century, warships were fitted with large guns, called cannons, to fire at enemy ships in an attempt to sink them. Today, warships can carry fighter planes and attack helicopters.

Glossary words

canal	dugout
coracle	reed boat

This painting shows an early Egyptian boat. Boats like this one were used along the Nile, Euphrates and Tigris rivers.

Explorers and trade

Explorers sailed ships all over the world looking for new land. As the explorers found new lands, more merchants began to trade for goods from these countries. Over time, all sorts of goods produced in foreign lands began to appear in countries thousands of miles away. For example, trading ships brought tea from China, sugar from the Caribbean, and spices and cotton from India to Britain. Today, huge container ships carry cargo in big metal boxes and ferry ships carry foot passengers, cars and trucks from one port to another.

Canal transport

People built a canal to transport goods from one place to another when there was no nearby river and the road system was not good enough. One of the oldest and longest canals in the world is the Grand Canal of China, which dates back to the 5th century BCE. The Suez Canal, which opened in 1869, connects the Mediterranean Sea to the Red Sea through the Isthmus of Suez in Egypt. It is 193.3 kilometres long and is used by about 17 000 ships a year.

Did you know?

On the River Nile, the wind always blows from north to south and the current always flows from south to north. So the sail could only be used when sailing in one direction. When travelling *against* the wind, the boat had to be rowed.

Activities

1. Explain how the following boats differ from each other: dugouts, coracles and reed boats.
2. Use the information in this book and further research to create a poster that explains how ships and boats were used for trade, exploration and war throughout history.

Challenge

Choose one type of ship (for example, a warship or a cruise liner). How has this type of ship changed since the first one was built? How has its use changed?

4.3 Rail transport

After the invention of the wheel, people made carts and carriages that were pulled by horses or donkeys. Over time, these wagons and carriages were pulled by animals on tracks or rails. The tracks allowed the wagons to move more quickly than on ordinary roads. These tracks were sometimes called railways. Who was the first person to use an engine on a railway? How did railways develop? Why are modern railways so important?

Early rail transport: horses pulling a carriage on rail tracks

Steam power

In 1804, Englishman Richard Trevithick attached a steam engine to a carriage that ran along a track. His locomotive, as it was called, pulled wagons that carried iron. Soon, other people began to use locomotives to transport heavy goods such as coal and iron. In 1808, Trevithick began charging passengers to travel on a wagon pulled by one of his locomotives.

Passenger locomotives

The world's first passenger railway opened in Britain in 1825. It ran a distance of 40 kilometres between two towns in the north of England. Soon there was a network of railways all over Britain. From the 1830s, railways started to spread throughout the world.

Be a good historian

Good historians are able to identify the consequences of an event, invention or development. Rail transport is a good example of how an invention and its further developments have had a major impact.

Trevithick's passenger train from 1808

Did you know?

The long trains that carry goods are called freight trains. The longest freight train ran in Australia in 2001. It was 7 kilometres long and had 682 wagons full of iron ore.

60

Impact of the locomotive

Locomotives and their railways changed the ways in which people lived and worked. People could work in the city but live in the country because the trains could transport thousands of people every day.

People and goods could be transported further and faster than ever before. Merchants and businesses used the railways to transport fresh food long distances quickly. A growing railway network created jobs, and also made towns, cities and countries much more connected with each other. For example, the Trans-Siberian Railway in Russia is over 9289 kilometres long and connects Moscow with the far east of Russia, Mongolia, China and North Korea.

Railway development meant that letters and newspapers could be delivered much more quickly so news spread faster. High-speed travel meant that sports clubs could now play teams from other places. In Britain, for example, a journey between London and Edinburgh took two weeks by road in 1745. By 1901, people could make the same journey in nine hours by rail.

Glossary words

freight train   Maglev
locomotive   railway

New locomotive power

By the 1950s, diesel engines were used more than steam engines in many countries. Diesel engines were easier to drive, quieter and cheaper to run than steam engines.

Some of the fastest locomotives today are powered by electricity. The fastest speed ever reached by an electric train was 574 kilometres per hour in France in 2007. In recent years, there has been an increase in the number of locomotives powered by magnets, particularly in Japan, Korea and China. They are called Maglevs and can travel at high speeds.

A Maglev in Shanghai

Activities

1. Prepare a lesson to teach younger students about the development and use of rail transport. Do some extra research and try to find out some advantages and disadvantages of rail transport.
2. Use books and the Internet to research how magnets are used to power locomotives. Write a short report about Maglevs.

Challenge

Find out how a steam engine works. Research the inventor of the steam engine and the people who helped improve it. Find out about the different ways in which steam engines were used in the past.

4.4 Up in the air

It is difficult to think of our world without air travel. Airplanes are a common sight in our skies. Every day thousands of airplanes carry people and cargo all over the world. How long have people been able to fly in machines in the sky? Who built the first airplane? How is air travel used today?

The first flights

In September 1783, French brothers Joseph and Étienne Montgolfier built a large balloon from cloth and paper. They lit a fire underneath the balloon that heated the air inside it. Hot air is lighter than cold air, so the balloon rose up from the ground. The first hot air balloon carried a sheep, a rooster and a duck for a mile. All the animals landed safely. A few months later, on 21 November, the brothers used their balloon to carry two men for five miles over Paris. It was a 25-minute flight. They were the first people ever to fly.

The first airplane

After the Montgolfier brothers, many other people experimented with flight. In 1852, airships were invented. The first airship was a balloon with a steam engine and propellers attached to steer the airship. In 1891, the first glider that could travel long distances and carry people was created.

The Montgolfier brothers' balloon

Then, on 17 December 1903, American brothers Orville and Wilbur Wright made the first engine-powered flight in an airplane. The flight lasted 12 seconds and covered a distance of 37 metres. By 1905, the brothers had made over 150 flights, some lasting nearly 40 minutes.

The development of air travel

During World War One (1914–18) airplanes were fitted with guns and bombs. After the war, airplanes were used to deliver goods from one place to another. In the 1920s, larger airplanes were built that could carry many passengers. These large airplanes are called airliners. Over time, airliners became bigger and could carry more and more passengers over greater distances.

Glossary words

airliner	glider
airship	perishable
cargo plane	

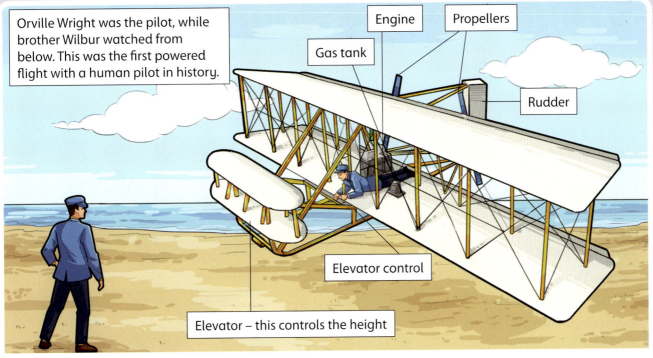

A diagram of the Wright brothers' airplane in flight

Air travel today

Today, air travel is one of the most popular ways to travel over long distances. The largest airliner is the Airbus A380-800, which can carry up to 853 people on two passenger floors. The Boeing 787-8 Dreamliner can fly up to 13 000 kilometres non-stop without refuelling. Huge airplanes, called cargo planes, transport perishable goods such as fruit, vegetables and flowers to markets thousands of miles away from where they are produced.

Activities

1. Make a timeline of the most important dates in the history of air travel. You will find lots of dates on these pages, but also carry out your own research.
2. Use the Internet and books to research modern hot air balloons and how these have developed since the Montgolfier brothers' first flight.

Challenge

Most airplanes today are powered by jet engines. Find out how about the history and development of the jet engine. Who invented the first jet engine? In what airplane was it first used? How does a jet engine works? Write a report about how a jet engine lifts an airplane into the sky.

Did you know?

Some airplanes can travel at twice the speed of sound. Sound travels at 343.2 metres per second, or 1 kilometre in 2.914 seconds.

4 A history of transport

63

4.5 Transport in the future

The ways in which we travel and transport goods are always changing. There are many new ideas and inventions in transport and travel. Recent developments include cars that can park themselves and goods that are delivered to your home by drone. What are the latest ideas and inventions in transport? Why has transport changed in recent years? How might transport develop in the future?

Space transport

Space transport is one of the newest types of transport. In 1961, Russian Yuri Gagarin became the first human in space when he orbited the Earth once during a 108-minute flight. In 1969, Americans Neil Armstrong and Buzz Aldrin became the first people to walk on the moon. In 1981, the Space Shuttle was launched. It was the first spaceship that could be reused many times. In 1998, the International Space Station (ISS) was put into orbit around the Earth.

The ISS is used as a research laboratory in which crew members conduct scientific experiments. Since 2000, permanent crews have been living and working on the ISS. The astronauts travel between Earth and the ISS in spacecraft. Space flight companies are now planning to offer tourist flights into space.

A model of how the first 'space tourism' spaceship might look

Environmentally friendly travel

Most cars, buses and trucks have engines that burn fuel made from oil. Some experts believe that the world's supply of fossil fuels (such as oil) is in short supply. Also, burning fossil fuels in engines releases polluting gases into the atmosphere, which has caused a number of serious environmental problems. As a result, engineers and designers are improving engines so they burn less fuel and developing new types of fuel and transport.

- Alternative fuel vehicles use energy that does not come from oil. For example, engines have been developed that use propane or vegetable oil.

Glossary words

drone   orbit

Did you know?

Driverless cars have been developed. These cars can drive safely behind other vehicles, detect buildings, stop suddenly for other cars and change speed.

Nissan's electric car 'Nissan Leaf' at the charging station in front of Nissan's global headquarters in Yokohama, Japan

- Walking and cycling not only protect the environment, but also get you fit.
- Using public transport (trains and buses) means there are fewer cars on the road, which in turn means less pollution.
- 'Smart cars' are becoming popular. Car-makers, including BMW and Nissan, are producing more electric smart cars fitted with many different types of technology to help the driver and to conserve energy. Smart cars use no petrol and operate for 130–160 kilometres per charge.

Be a good historian

Good historians know that, at any one time, some things are changing and some things are staying the same. Some changes happen quickly, triggered by new discoveries or changes in technology. Other changes happen slowly, especially if things have been done the same way for thousands of years.

Activities

1. Write a newspaper article called 'Transport in the future'. Include information from this book and any other information you can find out.
2. Create a fact file about the development of space travel – from the earliest attempts to reach space to the latest research carried out on the International Space Station (ISS).

Challenge

One of the most exciting new types of transportation under development is called hyperloop. Research hyperloop and write five interesting facts about it.

4 A history of transport

4 Review

Answer these questions in your notebook.

Choose the best answer from the choices below. Write a, b or c as your answer.

1. Most experts think the wheel was invented about:
   a 5000 years ago
   b 500 years ago
   c 50 years ago
2. The first wheels were made from:
   a stone
   b wood
   c metal
3. A trade route is:
   a a method of making goods quickly in a factory
   b a road used by Roman soldiers
   c a long network of roads that merchants use to transport goods
4. An internal combustion engine is:
   a a machine that harvests crops
   b an engine powered by burning petrol
   c an environmentally friendly electric engine
5. Ford Motor Company sold 15 million of which car between 1908 and 1927?
   a Model A
   b Model D
   c Model T

6. The world's first passenger railway opened in 1825 in:
   a England
   b France
   c Russia
7. The name given to long trains that carry goods is:
   a freight trains
   b Maglev trains
   c power trains
8. The names of the two American brothers who made the first engine-powered flight in an airplane were:
   a Robert and John Kennedy
   b Orville and Wilbur Wright
   c Joseph and Étienne Montgolfier

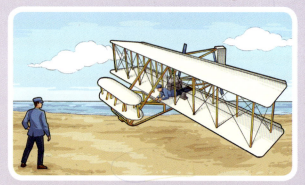

9. What is the name of cars that use many different types of technology to help the driver and conserve energy? These cars consume no petrol and operate for 130–160 kilometres per charge.
   a clever cars
   b sharp cars
   c smart cars

Decide if these statements are true or false. Write 'True' or 'False' for each one.

10 The first hot air balloon journey carried Joseph and Étienne Montgolfier.

11 A Maglev train is powered by magnets and can travel at high speeds.

12 A car that has an electric motor for short journeys and a petrol engine for longer journeys is called a hybrid.

Now complete these tasks.

13 Write an information sheet about the following types of boat:
   a dugouts
   b coracles
   c reed boats

Include information about where and when they were used and the similarities and differences between them.

14 Carry out a survey to find out what types of transport people in your class have used. Ask what types of transport they use most often, as well as the different types of transport they have used in their lifetime. Present your findings using charts and graphs.

15 Create a single timeline showing developments in transport. Include developments in road, rail, air and sea transport.

Vocabulary quiz

Answer these questions in your notebook.

1 Roman invasion

1 Choose the words to label this picture of a Roman soldier.

armour   helmet   sandals
shield   skirt   spear   sword

2 Write a definition for each of the following words. Then use each word correctly in a sentence or short paragraph.
   a empire
   b conquer
   c invade
   d basilica
   e literate
   f pension

2 The Anglo-Saxons

1 Look at the picture of an Anglo-Saxon house. Write the labels for a, b and c.

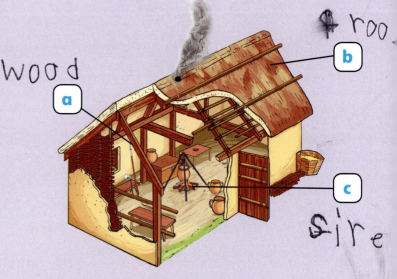

2 Choose the word that matches each definition.
   a armour made from metal rings that are joined together to form a protective cover

   chariot   chain mail   conquer

   b to attack quickly and unexpectedly to steal things

   settle   raid   conquer

   c a group of the king's advisors

   Celts   ceorls   witan

3 Which is the odd one out in each group of words? Explain your answer.
   a king   thane   pottage   ceorl
   b Germany   Denmark   Spain   Netherlands
   c Northumbria   Scotland   Mercia   Wessex

68

3 The Maya

1 Match the words with the definitions.
   a the plant that produces corn (or sweetcorn)
   b an ancient manuscript in book form
   c flat areas cut into a hillside for growing crops
   d a place or building used for making observations of the stars and planets

   > codex   maize
   > observatory   terraces

2 a Sort the words below in a table.

Found in a city	Mayan achievements	People in Mayan society

   > ball court   farms   slaves
   > nobles   pyramids   mathematics
   > king   astronomy   glyphs

   b Add one new word to each group.

3 Write what each of these pictures shows. Then use each word correctly in a sentence or short paragraph.

a

b

c
fire   cloud

4 A history of transport

1 Match the words with the definitions.
   a the use of science to invent new things or to solve problems
   b something used for transporting people or goods
   c a way of putting together a product in a factory by moving it along a line of workers
   d the process of growing or progressing

   > development   vehicle
   > assembly line   technology

2 Which is the odd one out in each group of words? Explain your answer.
   a Fiat Ford Rolls-Royce Wright
   b chariot dugout reed boat coracle
   c airship balloon airliner locomotive

3 Write what each of these pictures shows. Then use each word correctly in a sentence or short paragraph.

a

b

c

Glossary

airliner a large airplane that can carry many passengers

airship a large balloon filled with gas or air and driven by engines

aqueduct a bridge with a stone channel to carry fresh water into towns from a river or lake

archeologist a person who studies past human life, by looking at objects and other evidence

armour clothing that is worn to protect the body

assassinate to murder an important person, usually for political or religious reasons

assembly line a way of putting together a product in a factory by moving it along a line of workers. Each worker adds or adjusts a part until the product is finished.

astronomy the scientific study of stars, planets and other objects in space

auxiliary a type of Roman soldier

ballista a large, powerful crossbow

barbarians the name given to tribes that the Romans considered to be uncivilised

bartering exchanging goods without using money

battering ram a heavy object swung or rammed against a door or wall to break it down

basilica a Roman building used as a council chamber and law court

canal a waterway built to allow boats or ships to travel from one place to another

cargo plane an airplane that transports goods around the world

cavalry soldiers on horses

Celts tribes who lived in Britain at the time of the Roman invasion. The Romans called these people 'Britons', not Celts.

centurion the soldier in charge of a century

century a group of 80 men in the Roman army; a period of 100 years

ceorl an ordinary villager in Anglo-Saxon society

chain mail armour made from metal rings that are joined together to form a protective cover

chariot a fast, light, two-wheeled vehicle pulled by horses

city-state a city and the area of land around it

civilisation a large, organised group of people who live and work together in the same region

codex an ancient manuscript in book form

conquer to defeat, usually in a war or a battle

coracle a light, round boat made by sewing animal skins over a wooden frame

craftsperson a person who is skilled at a craft, such as jewellery-making, furniture-making or metal-working

culture the ideas, customs and behaviour of a group of people, shown in everything from language, food and clothing through to art, music and literature

Danelaw an area of Britain controlled by the Vikings

development the process of growing or progressing

drone an unmanned aircraft, usually flown by remote control but which can also fly using on-board sensors and GPS

dugout a small boat made by hollowing out a tree trunk

empire an area, usually comprising many countries, ruled by an emperor or empress

environmentally friendly not harmful to the environment

event something important that happens

forum the market place or public square in a Roman city; a place of assembly for the people

freight train a long train that transports goods

glider a light aircraft designed to fly without using an engine

goods things that people trade, for example food, tools, clothing and luxury items

governor an important Roman official in charge of a conquered country

hieroglyphics a system of writing that uses pictures to represent words, sounds and objects

invade to enter, using force

invention a new process or object that did not previously exist

kingdom an area, or country, ruled by a king or queen

legion a large group within the Roman army

legionary the best and highest-paid type of Roman soldier

literate able to read and write

literature written works, especially ones of lasting value such as novels, poems, historical accounts and essays

locomotive the engine that provides the power to pull carriages or wagons

longboat a long, narrow boat used by the Vikings

Maglev a train powered by magnets

maize the plant that produces corn (or sweetcorn)

material what something is made of

nobles a powerful group in Mayan society who helped the king to run the city-state

nutrients things needed by people, plants and animals to help them grow

observatory a place or building used for making observations of the stars and planets

occupation a period of time when a country is controlled by military force

onager a machine that was used to throw large rocks

orbit to move around a star or planet

pension a regular payment given as a reward for doing a job for a long time

perishable likely to decay or go bad quickly

pottage a thick soup

pyramid a building with triangular sides, used by the Maya as a tomb for dead kings and for public ceremonies

raid a surprise attack to steal objects, animals or people or to destroy property; to attack quickly and unexpectedly to steal or to destroy property

railway the tracks on which a locomotive and carriages travel

rebel to rise in opposition or armed resistance against a government or leader

record to write about events so people will know about them in the future

reed boat a boat made from reeds (long grass) found near rivers

reign the period of rule of a king or queen

settle to stay and live in a place

social class a group of people who all have a similar level of wealth, influence and status

society a large group of people who live in an organised way

squash a type of vegetable-like fruit, for example pumpkins and courgettes

stagecoach a coach which travelled from one place to another and stopped during the journey for fresh horses and food for the passengers

stepped farming a type of farming that uses steps built into the side of a mountain or hill. Crops are planted on each level.

symbol a written character that represents a letter, number or whole word

tax payment demanded by a ruler or government

technology the use of science to invent new things or to solve problems

terrace a flat area cut into a hillside for growing crops

textiles woven or knitted cloth

thane one of the king's most trusted advisors in Anglo-Saxon society

thatched covered with straw or rushes to make a roof

the past all the time before now

timeline a way of showing events in order of when they happened, along a line

tomb a special chamber for burying the dead

tortilla a thin, flat bread made from maize flour

trade buying and selling goods

trade route a long network of roads that merchants and traders used to transport goods between one place and another. Some trade routes were over the sea.

tribe a group of families and relatives who have the same customs and beliefs

vehicle something used for transporting people or goods

witan the advisors of an Anglo-Saxon king